# Regency
# Women's Dress

# Regency
# Women's Dress

Cassidy Percoco

Costume & Fashion Press / QSM
Los Angeles

First published in the United Kingdom in 2015 by
Batsford
1 Gower Street
London WC1E 6HD
An imprint of Pavilion Books Company Ltd
www.pavilionbooks.com

Reproduction by COLOURDEPTH, UK
Printed and bound by Toppan Leefung
Printing Ltd, China

First published in the United States of America
by Costume & Fashion Press / QSM
An imprint of
Silman-James Press, Inc.
info@silmanjamespress.com
www.silmanjamespress.com

ISBN: 978-0-89676-297-8

10 9 8 7 6 5 4 3 2 1

# Contents

# Introduction

The Regency period proper began in 1811, with the appointment of the future King George IV, the Prince of Wales, as Prince Regent; it ended in 1820, when he came to the throne. However, the term 'Regency period' – or the more accurate 'long Regency' – is often used to refer to the later 1790s and the first three decades of the nineteenth century. The dress of this period was characterized by raised waistlines, narrower skirts, and historical influences on fashion; outside of dress, it was knitted together with the upheavals in French politics, the early Romantic movement in poetry and literature, and its similarity in manners and mores as contrasted with those of the Victorian era.

The history of the dress of this period is not well known, often even among fashion historians. It is stereotyped as very high waistlines, white muslin and bonnets – but there was a significant amount of fluctuation and change. For historians and curators, it is important to be able to date garments and portraits in museum collections accurately, in order to keep records well and to determine whether or not the given provenance for an object is likely to be correct. For those who make re-creations of historical dress for film or reenactment, accuracy is less vital but an entertaining aspect of the pastime.

The patterns in this book span the first three decades of the nineteenth century, and have been drawn from garments in smaller museums in New York state. Previous collections of patterns that have included this era, such as Norah Waugh's *The Cut of Women's Clothes* and Janet Arnold's *Patterns of Fashion I*, cover a longer period of time and therefore can devote less space to each sub-period: *Regency Women's Dress*, containing 26 patterns, is able to show a far greater amount of variation within these decades. The garments, being mainly of American origin, provide a much-needed resource for American academics, who have previously only worked with patterns of British origin. While some aspects of construction and style are near-universal for most Western countries during this time period, there are certain stylistic divergences between Britain and France, in which American women tended to side with their French cousins.

On the patterns, each block in the grid is equivalent to 1in (2.5cm) on the original. The method of scaling up patterns for sewing use preferred by the author is to use the grid as a guide and draw out the individual pieces on a sheet of newsprint or oversized paper, measuring up, down, and over from a set of points. Alternatively the patterns can be enlarged on a photocopier.

# A History of Regency Dress

During the early nineteenth century, 'morning' was the time between breakfast (usually held sometime between 8am and 10am) and dinner (between 4pm and 7pm): while at home in the morning, a woman would wear a morning dress (*robe du matin*) or undress (*négligée*) of an inexpensive fabric like a cotton print or linen, generally with long sleeves, a higher neckline, and a concealing cap. If she were to go out walking or to pay calls, she would put on walking or visiting dress – something of a more expensive fabric, with more embellishment, with a hat or bonnet. If riding, she would wear a riding habit (*amazone*) made of wool in a dark or drab colour.

A woman might wear full dress or half dress to dinner, depending on the level of formality required: if only the family were dining, if guests were to be present, and so on. Ball dresses (*robes du bal*) were shorter than full dress, since they were worn for dancing, and during much of this period they were often a light sheer silk fabric, such as gauze or crepe, worn over a taffeta or satin slip (*dessous*) in either white or the colour of the gown. Flowers, both real and artificial, were often used as decorations both in the hair and on the ball dress.

A timeline of women's clothing and accessories in the most detailed particulars could occupy the space of dozens of pages, but here I present a shortened version based on my research on extant gowns and French and English fashion plates.

The white muslin chemise gown – loose, draped and fitted mainly by drawstrings – became fashionable in the later 1780s, and when the waistline rose in the mid-1790s the gowns took on an even more Hellenistic air. This was deliberate: Neoclassicism had been in vogue for furniture and architecture for some time, as well as philosophy and political thought, and the time was ripe

for it to be expressed through women's dress. With the higher waist came a new form of stays, shortened at the bottom but at first essentially the same shape as those of the rest of the eighteenth century; fairly soon they developed shaping to give the bust a more rounded and raised appearance, usually separating the breasts far more than is fashionable today. In keeping with the prevailing attitude that a natural beauty was better than the artifices of cosmetics, hooped petticoats or false rumps, fashionable hair could be dressed without powder and with long curls cut in varying layers and a fringe hanging over the forehead. It might also be twisted up into a chignon with loose ends visible at the top of the head, or 'cropt' short into a cut *à la Titus* – a very modern-looking style that nonetheless persisted in fashion through the first decade of the nineteenth century: Jane Austen complained of her niece Anna's 'sad cropt head' in 1808 and 1809.

White was the most fashionable colour for gowns during the late 1790s, often trimmed with bright colours along the hemline and at the ends of the fitted, elbow-length sleeves. White appeared to be the colour of the drapery on Classical statues, it was cool in the summer, it matched all coloured accessories, and it was difficult to keep clean, which gave it an added status boost. The fabric of some white gowns was embroidered on the loom with repeated white motifs, or printed with a geometric pattern. Cotton prints were used, as were coloured silk, but in the most fashionable dress coloured fabrics (generally wool or cashmere) were reserved for outerwear: pelisses (*redingotes*), long overgowns styled like men's coats, generally buttoning in front; spencers, jackets that ended at the high waist; *douillettes*, lighter pelisses that were often shorter than the gowns beneath them, and were styled like gowns; and *witzchouras*, heavier and looser than pelisses, usually with a fur lining and a hood. Accessories like shawls (square or rectangular), leather shoes, hats and turbans, and ribbon belts also were coloured. One particular style of ribbon belt wrapped around the shoulders and crossed over the back – originally blood red, it was called the *ceinture à la victime* after the victims of the guillotine, and in various colours it continued to be worn to about 1810.

Some accessories, however, were generally white: the chemisette (*guimpe*) filled in or covered the neckline of a gown like a sleeveless, short shirt and held a ruffled collar (a *demi-guimpe* had no collar); the *canezou* was a light muslin spencer.

The chemise or round gown of the late 1790s and early 1800s generally had a fitted back, and fastened in the front at neck and waist with drawstrings. Open robes that were cut more like earlier eighteenth century gowns, open in the skirt to show a (white) petticoat, were a more formal choice, with noblewomen described in magazines as wearing them to great occasions.

In French fashion (which was followed in America), the train began to disappear from day dress just a few years into the new century, then from evening dress; by 1806, evening dress was actually slightly shorter than day dress. Both were cut with skirt shaping to flare at the ankle. More recent historical inspiration than the Greeks and Romans was also coming into vogue which inspired aspects such as fuller sleeves from 1804, soon turning into round puffs (and puffed, short oversleeves over long undersleeves); trim running down the front of the gown and around the hem (*à la Reine Mathilde*) from 1803 to 1808; and a large, pleated white muslin frill worn around the neck from 1803 was named for several different historical figures before it simply became commonplace.

British dress differed from that of the French and Americans from the beginning of the century. The Neoclassical influence held strong, with trains remaining in everyday fashion until 1809 (they continued in evening and full dress until 1813),

skirts being cut from straighter panels, and fitted sleeves holding sway. This was not an effect of distance or political opposition, but simply a difference in national tastes. The English fashion magazine *La Belle Assemblée* was reproducing French fashion plates from a few months to a year after they were published across the Channel in the *Journal des Dames et des Modes*, even several years into the Napoleonic wars. During the Peninsular campaign and the war of 1812 there was undoubtedly a political component to the choice of British or French fashion, but as dress travelled as fast as a package or letter in the post, the issue was not of anyone being 'cut off' from their preferred source.

From the beginning of the century, a rounded neckline – tightened on the drawstring – was the most common, but it was superseded around 1804 (first in France, then in Britain) by a squared neckline created with separate shoulder straps and a rectangular piece as the front of the bodice. The bottom of the neckline was often on a drawstring, but as it did not include the sides the corners were preserved. A sweetheart neckline (called *en coeur* in French) began to appear at the same time, deepening to a V neckline (also called *en coeur*) and becoming somewhat common around 1808 – especially in Britain – then persisting for many years. Another persistent style, first appearing in 1809, was a bodice pleated horizontally across the bust, with a band running down the centre; later it would be called a bodice *à la Sevigné*.

While British dress tended to leave the skirt completely unadorned during the 1800s, French women added a ruffle, embroidery, or a ribbon in a fabric casing to the hem which emphasised the width and flare of the skirt. This trim became heavier and then subsided again as skirts became narrower at the end of the decade, as in British fashion. Scalloped hems began to appear around this time, and they continued despite the narrowing of the skirt.

The short corsets of the Neoclassical transition period did not last very long. By 1806, English women had a choice between long and short corsets; in 1808, French women were also wearing a new style of corset (called there a *corset à la Medicis*) that covered and smoothed the stomach and hips due to the narrowness of the gown. The earlier gowns, which were gathered across the front on drawstrings, hid most physical imperfections, and the fashionable body was curved and full; when the bodice began to be fitted and the skirt attached without gathering or pleats in front, the fashionable body was slim and lithe and more stomach control was necessary.

Necklines were quite commonly low in day and evening dress (though lower in France), but in the early 1810s a higher and wide neckline became a common aspect of day dress. Sleeves also became smaller: the puffed orbs of evening dress shrank closer to the shoulder, and while long sleeves might be loose, they lost their short oversleeves.

Skirts in France began to widen again at the ankle, where they were often trimmed to a larger height than before, with heavy embroidery or multiple rows of ruffles, casings, pintucks or other embellishments. They also began to shrink in daywear, hitting the middle of the ankle or higher by 1813. In Britain, skirts remained long and unadorned until about 1813, when the skirts of morning and walking dresses quickly shrank and took on narrow or wide bands of trim. These flared skirts generally had a fullness at the back not unlike a small bustle. The short, puffed oversleeves began to reappear by 1816.

The fashionable neckline for formal dress in the 1810s was broad and low, and in morning dress it could be either close to the neck or high and wide. A very wide neckline began to be common even in demure morning dress, and a higher one even in the most daring ball gown, from 1817; these were more often accentuated with a trim or collar. In the early 1820s, the neckline slipped even more toward the point of the shoulder, pushing the armhole lower and the sleeve as well. This created a more horizontal effect, the neckline and the top of the puffed sleeve being on the same level. By 1824, the puffs were slightly more exaggerated in the middle, creating a slight angle. By this point,

long sleeves were still generally fitted, with puffed oversleeves to give them volume, but later that year long sleeves that were themselves puffed at the top and tapering to the wrist were introduced, and these continued in use as the morning counterparts to the short but wide sleeves seen on evening dress. They remained roughly the same size until the very end of the decade, when they ballooned out to great proportions.

Waists were extremely high in the earlier 1810s, hitting just at the bottom of the bust. They were, however, to decline not long after: by 1819, the waist tended to be an inch (2.5cm) or even two lower, and continued to get slightly lower every few years, until by 1829 it reached the natural level or slightly below it. Bonnet crowns lowered as well and the brims widened, then the crown rose again in narrow towers for the broad-brimmed hats popular at the end of the 1820s.

As the waist lowered, the cut of the skirt changed little. Skirts might, however, be sewn flat to the bodice further around the waist in order to pull the fabric closer to the wearer's hips, and the embellishments on the hem were more intricate: puffed and gathered lengths of fabric, hundreds of little silk leaves arranged in patterns or narrow ruched strips, for example. Around 1820 the dress might be worn with more petticoats in order to hold out the skirt, and by 1822 padded hems and trims were being used to give it more body; it was not until later in the decade that skirts were being cut with less-gored panels requiring more shaping through pleating at the waist, even on the front of the gown. By this time, the trims on the skirt were frequently less intricate but usually higher, at or above the level of the knee.

The fashions of the beginning of the nineteenth century signalled an enormous break with the dress that came before them, which had been almost unchanged in fundamentals for the entire previous century. However, once the great transition had been accomplished, they continued to progress in a slightly quicker manner than they had before, the changes picking up speed into the beginning of the Victorian era.

# Chemise
## 1800–1820

At the beginning of the century, geometric shirt and chemise construction was still commonly used. The front and back of this chemise are each made from a single length of fabric, cut with slanted sides in order to flare out. They are attached via shoulder straps, folded in half, with the fold placed along the neckline. The

sleeves, almost rectangles with a slightly curved head, are sewn to square godets, then set into the chemise so that the seam allowance is sandwiched into the straps. The sleeves are whipped to the strap at each gather (a technique known as 'stroked gathers'); even the flat portions are sewn with whipstitches.

The side seams are sewn with alternating running and backstitches, then felled with an underhand hem stitch. The neckline edges of the body pieces are hemmed before the straps are attached: the body pieces lap the straps by 12mm (½in) and are backstitched in place, while the edges of the straps are turned under and whipped down. The hem is sewn with an underhand hem stitch. In this example, a 'G' is cross stitched in red thread inside the centre-front neck.

Left: *Chemise courtesy of the Albany Institute of History and Art, Albany, NY (X1940.54.5 1898.1.2). This detail shows the cross-stitched 'G' in the interior front neckline.*

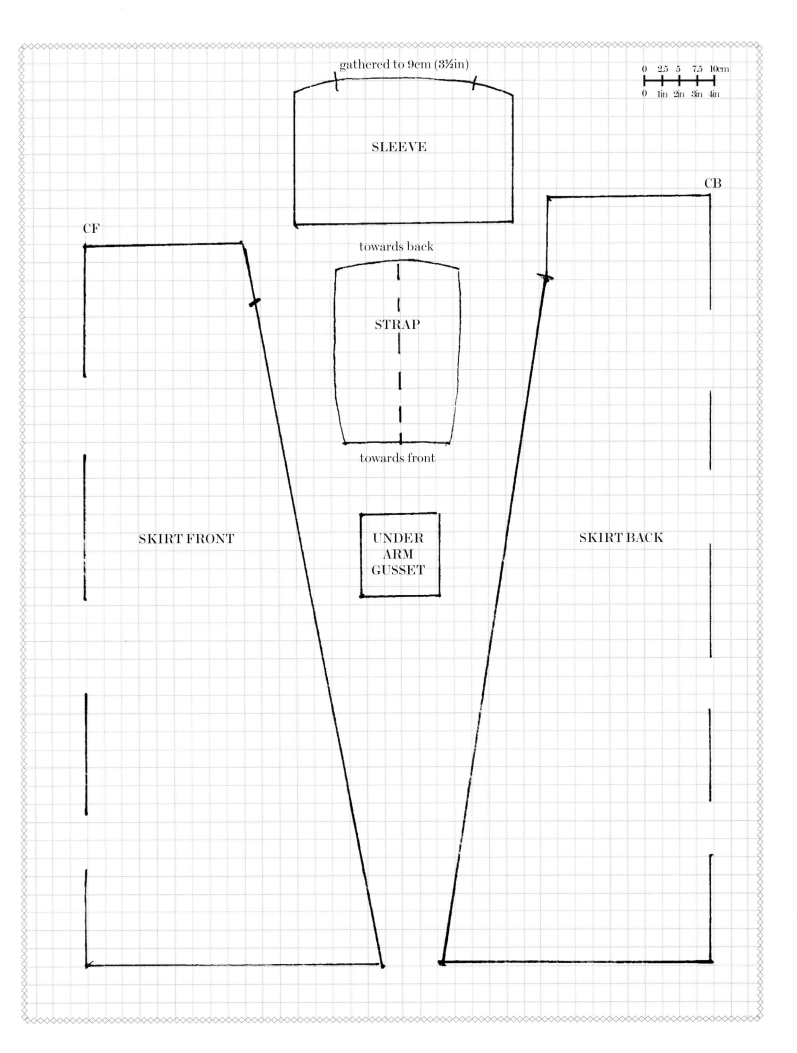

# Chemise
## 1820–1840

Later chemises began to incorporate greater sleeve shaping. As with the previous chemise, this one has flared body pieces in front and back. Around the sleeve attachment, the body is reinforced on the inside, front and back, with trapezoidal pieces as shown. The front neckline is gathered to 33cm (13in); the left side of the back to 11.5cm (4½in), and the right to 13cm (5in).

The sleeve head gathers are slightly lighter for the first few inches in front.

The neckline edge of the chemise is bound with a 104cm (41in) length of cotton, which is 1.5cm (⁵/₈in) wide when folded. On the right side of the back, the binding holds a buttonhole; on the left, a small mother-of-pearl button. A strip of the same width binds the gathered bottom edges of the sleeves.

The chemise was owned by a Rachel Ann Williams. The initials 'RWI' are cross-stitched in light blue at the center front of the body, just below the binding.

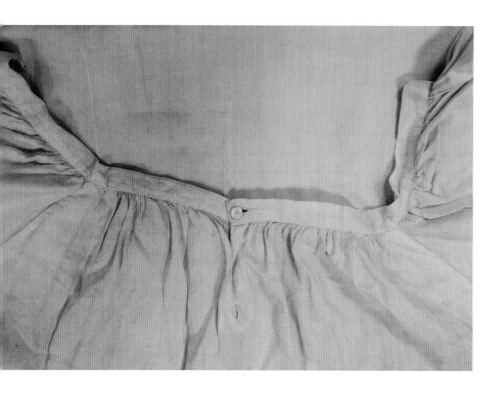

*Left: Chemise with gathered sleeves courtesy of the Albany Institute of History and Art, Albany, NY (1954.17.3). This detail shows the fastening at the back neckline.*

Regency Women's Dress

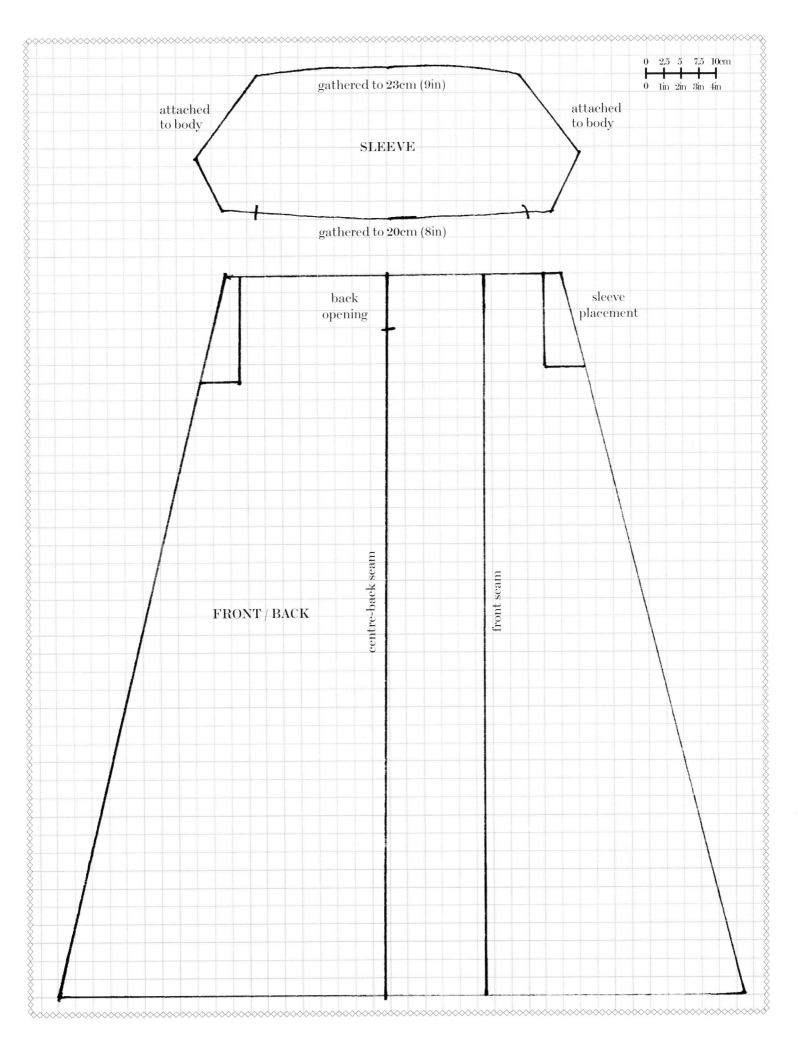

gathered to 23cm (9in)

attached to body

attached to body

SLEEVE

gathered to 20cm (8in)

back opening

sleeve placement

centre-back seam

front seam

FRONT / BACK

0   2.5   5   7.5   10cm

0   1in   2in   3in   4in

# Short stays
## 1795–1805

These short stays were cut and sewn much the same as earlier stays had been, but were much shorter and lighter. Made of a heavy white linen with no lining, all of the seams are sewn by turning the allowances between the pieces and whipping them together. The channels were backstitched, either before or after the piecing was done. The narrow back pieces flare out into the small of the back due to the angled cut of the centre-back seam.

The top edge of the fronts and backs of the stays is, as with the seams, turned in and hidden. Under the arms, the edge is covered with a leather binding, as is the entire lower edge of the stays. The straps, two layers of a slightly finer linen, were added roughly, sewn to the interior of the stays with little finishing.

The front lacing would allow the wearer to put on her stays more easily by herself without help.

Right: *Short stays courtesy of the New York State Historical Association, Cooperstown, NY (N391.67), showing the interior of left side.*

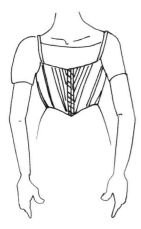

Right: *Illustration by J. Green from* Poetical Sketches of Scarborough *(1813) showing the shorter-style stays. The front lacing allows the wearer to put on her stays by herself – as this young lady was no doubt attempting before she was interrupted at her bath.*

Regency Women's Dress

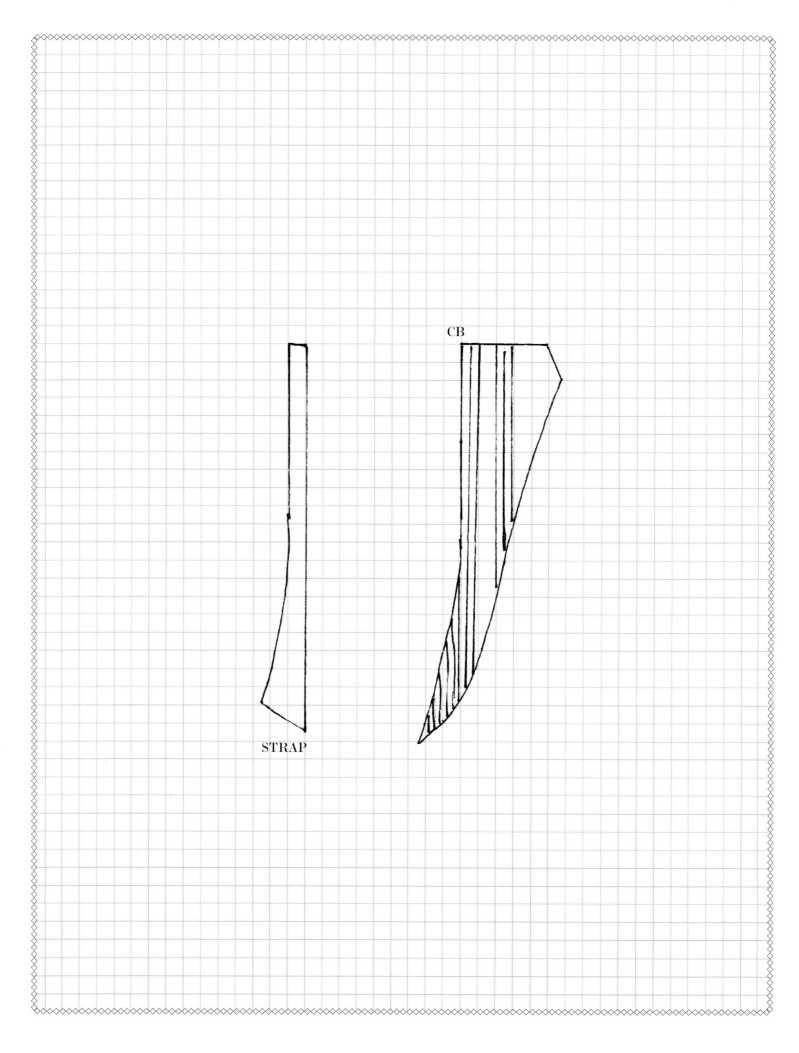

CB

STRAP

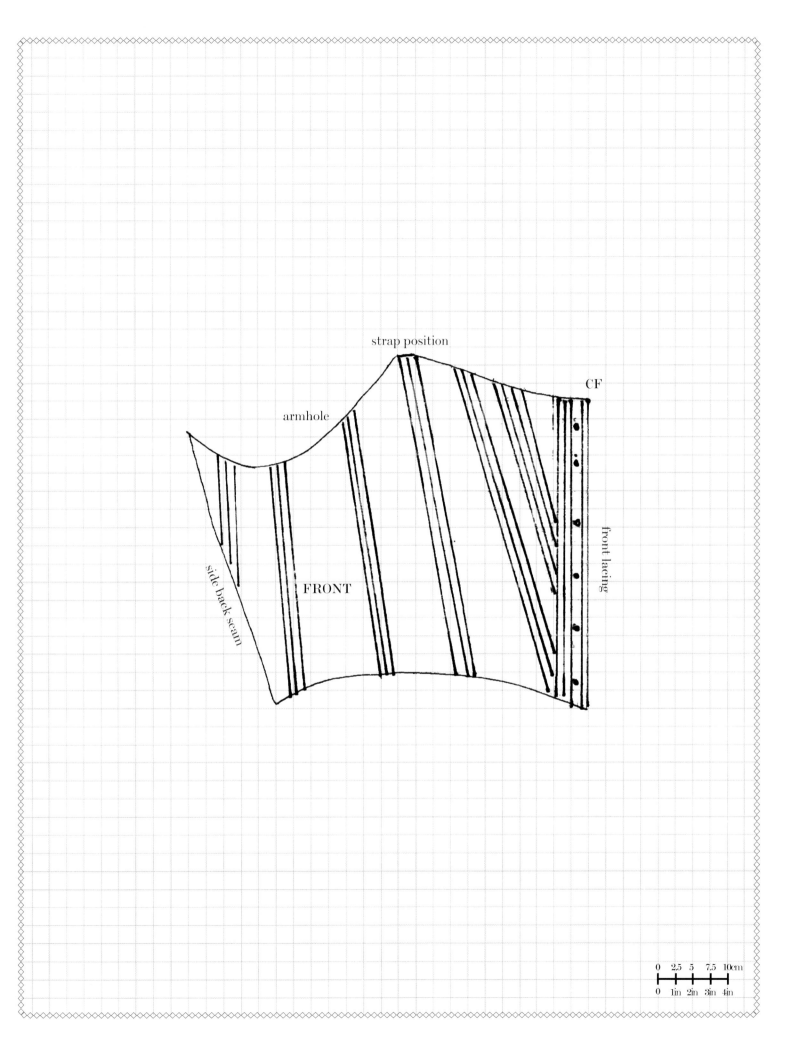

strap position

armhole

CF

side back seam

FRONT

front lacing

| 0 | 2.5 | 5 | 7.5 | 10cm |

| 0 | 1in | 2in | 3in | 4in |

# Corset
## 1805–1815

Longer corsets of this type were taken up not long after the turn of the century, and were worn for several decades, not falling out of use until the 1850s, when the popularization of the split busk made it even easier for a woman to put on or remove her corset herself. The shape gave a smooth line to the body and bust support, but without the vertical channels for whalebone that had been a necessity in creating the eighteenth century silhouette. Very little seaming was required: as with this example, the entire body of the corset could be cut in one piece, with triangular gussets added at the bust and hips to create the garment's shaping, and straps added at the shoulders – a requirement for this type of corset, as the lack of boning (apart from the wooden busk running down the centre front) meant that the bust needed the support of straps, like a modern bra. The gussets are all topstitched over the body of the corset on the outside, while the body is topstitched over the straps; the gussets in the lining are whipped over the body lining, and the straps under.

While earlier stays tended to be made from linen canvas, corsets in this style were usually a cotton twill. This corset is made from brown cotton twill, and lined with a plain-woven white cotton.

Most early nineteenth century corsets make significant use of cording and/or quilting. This one is topstitched in white and brown silk thread in the zigzagged pattern down the busk pocket (the lining is itself quilted with running stitches down the length of the pocket), in the angled lines across the midsection, spaced 6mm (¼in) apart, and in the curved lines next to the row of eyelets in the back. As time went on and a narrower waist became more desirable, it became common for the corset to be more heavily reinforced with cording across the hips and around the waist.

The upper edge of the corset is turned down and piped, with the back edge of the busk pocket turned in separately to facilitate adding or removing the busk. The lower edges are turned between the layers and whipped together. The curved centre-back edge is corded in two rows next to the eyelets, all of which are sewn in brown silk thread.

At the Xs are sewn downward-pointing metal eyes. These were likely used to hold a petticoat fitted with matching hooks: the only other way to hold a petticoat up to the high waistline would be to attach straps to it.

Left: *Brown corset courtesy of the New York State Historical Association, Cooperstown, NY (N506.61).*

Right: *A young French lady is fitted with a fashionable corset in* La Madame de Corsets *by Numa (c.1830). Corsets that laced up the back really required the help of a maid. You can see from this illustration how difficult the process would be without one.*

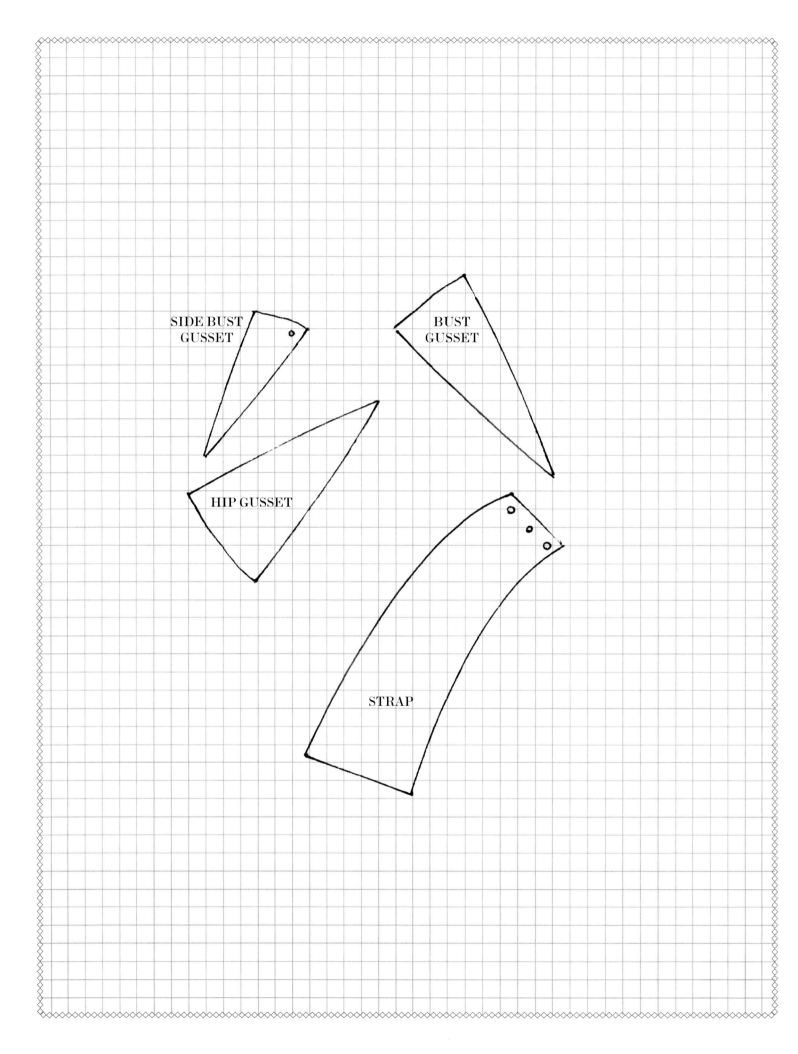

SIDE BUST
GUSSET

BUST
GUSSET

HIP GUSSET

STRAP

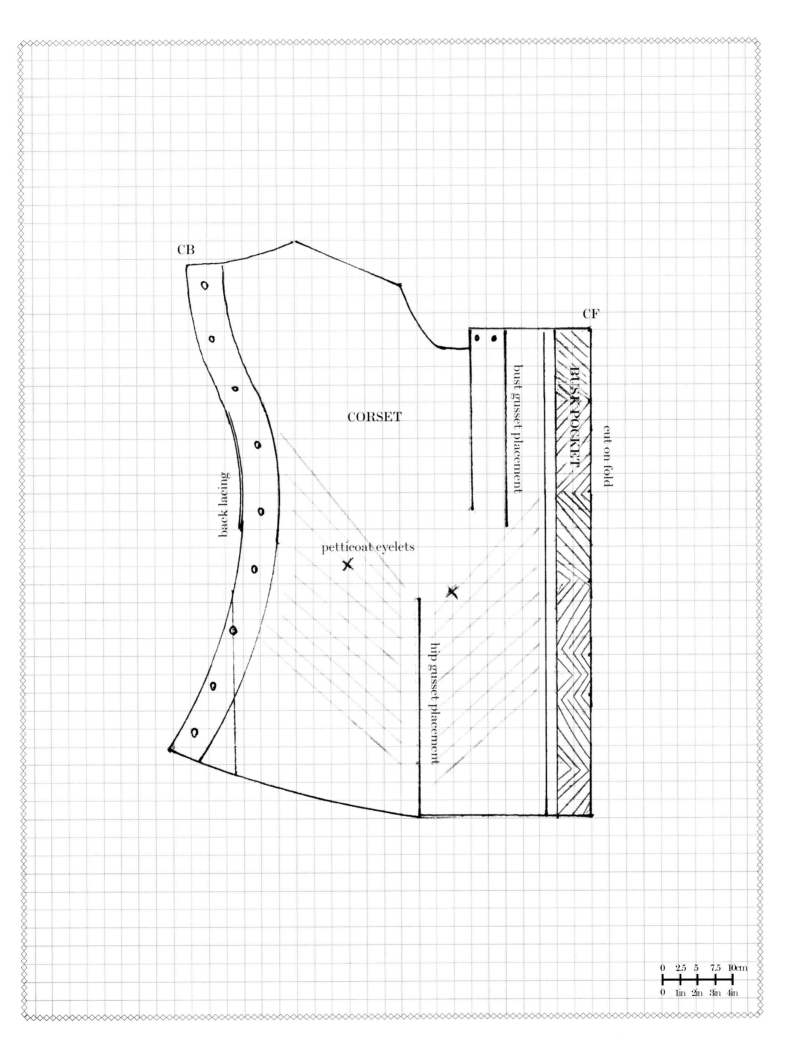

CB

CF

CORSET

back lacing

bust gusset placement

BUSK POCKET

cut on fold

petticoat eyelets

hip gusset placement

0   2.5   5   7.5   10cm

0   1in   2in   3in   4in

# Morning Jacket (*Camisole*)
## 1800–1815

This jacket was likely worn with a matching ruffled petticoat. The fabric is a heavy white cotton; the seams are backstitched with cotton thread, the raw seam allowances overcast, and the edges hemmed with an underhand hem stitch. The centre-back seam, however, is made of two selvedges whipped together. 'HMVR', the initials of the original owner, a woman of the van Rensselaer family, are cross-stitched in silk inside the dotted rectangle on the left-back piece, each stitch running over two threads in either direction. The silk has faded to a greyish mauve colour.

The collar is attached with the seam allowances on the outside and flat felled. The collar's buttonhole is only on the left side: no button remains on the other. Only the left sleeve is pieced: the long, straight seam in the centre of the sleeve is made by whipping two selvedges together, while the edges on the horizontal seam are hemmed and then whipped together.

The ties are a single layer of cotton, hemmed narrowly at the edges, each 4cm (1½in) wide and 56cm (22in) long. The channel, demarcated by broken lines, is applied on the inside, with buttonholes at the ends on the outside. Each tie is sewn into one end of the channel, extending from the opposite buttonhole to tie in front.

A lighter cotton ruffle edges the opening and lower edge of the jacket, with another around the collar and two more on the ends of the sleeves. These ruffles are 3cm (1¼in) wide and are gathered and attached with neat whipstitching.

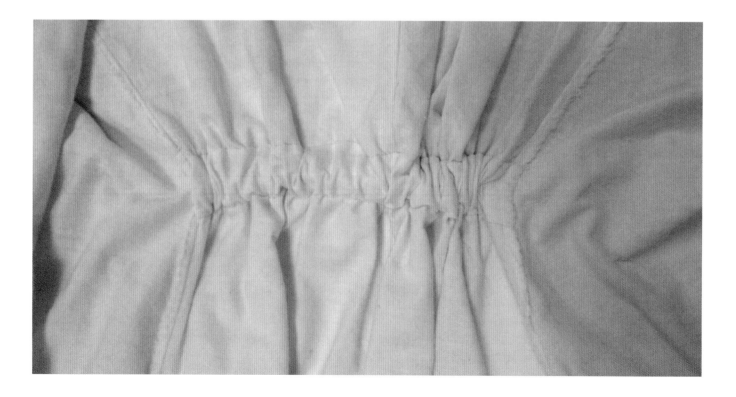

Left: *Simple morning jacket courtesy of the Historic Cherry Hill Collection, Albany, NY (3646). This detail shows where the ties gather at the back waist.*

Right: *Morning dresses illustrated in* Lady's Magazine, *1803. The gowns of white muslin are worn with fur-trimmed pelisses, one of which has a wrap over front.*

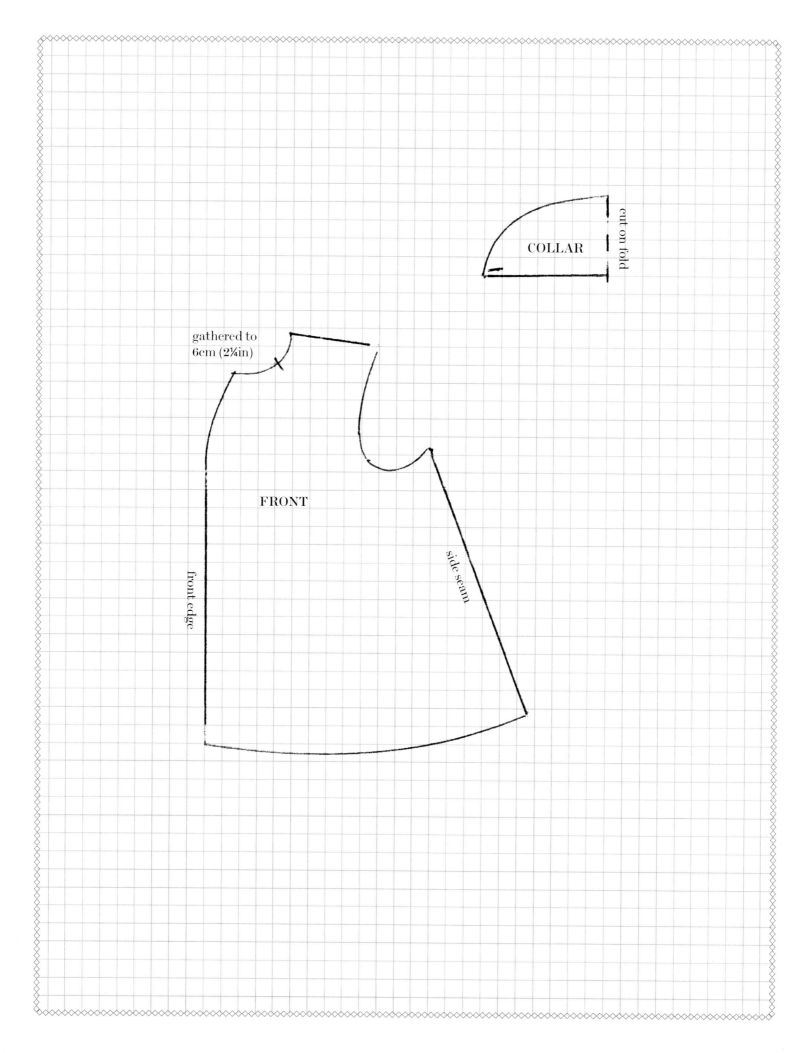

COLLAR

cut on fold

gathered to
6cm (2¼in)

FRONT

front edge

side seam

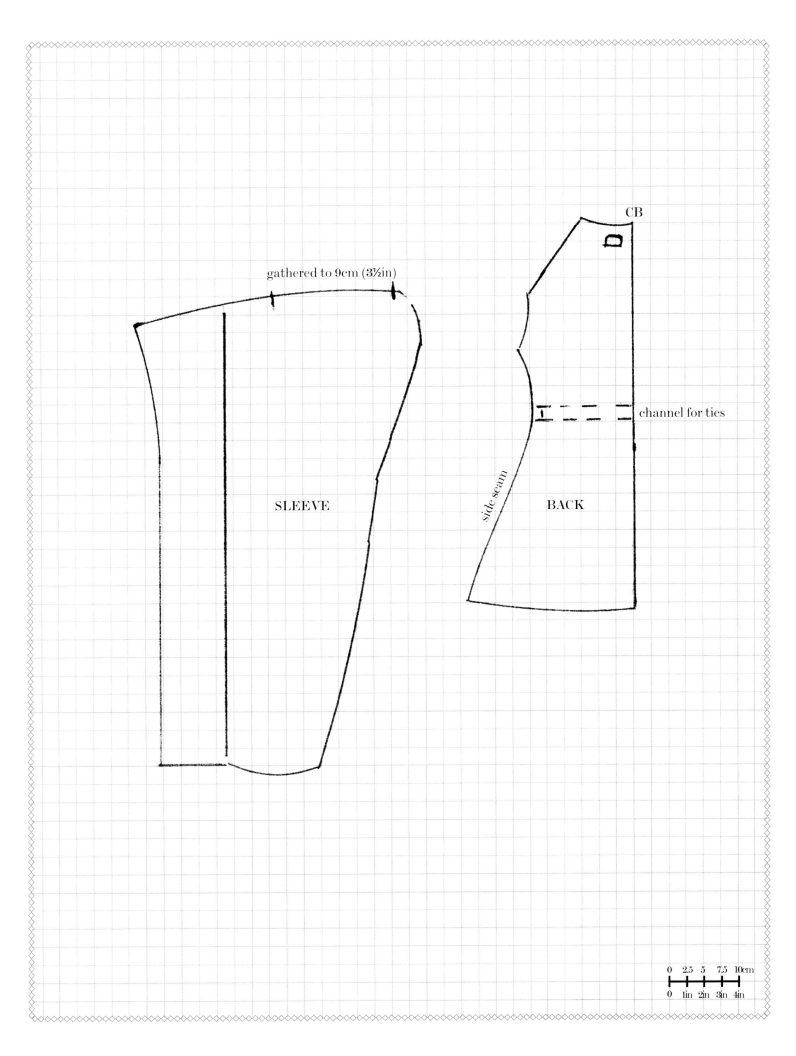

gathered to 9cm (3½in)

CB

channel for ties

SLEEVE

side seam

BACK

| 0 | 2.5 | 5 | 7.5 | 10cm |

| 0 | 1in | 2in | 3in | 4in |

# Spencer
## 1797–1810

The spencer was originally a man's tailless overcoat, and was brought into women's dress in the late 1790s. At that time, the lapels of the original garment were retained, as were buttoning cuffs. This spencer is made from a heavy silk with a brown velvet stripe, of the type that was frequently used for men's coats. It is lined with a mustard yellow silk taffeta – possibly a re-purposing of an old gown, as the colour had been popular several decades before.

The entire lining was sewn together with white silk thread; the striped silk was not topstitched through it, so it is likely that it was also sewn together separately. The only structural topstitching is on the pleat under the arm down to the mark, which is done in brown silk, the inner edge of the pleat being sewn to the lining with white thread. The body is faced with striped silk to the broken line on the front edge for lapels, and the lining only extends down to the broken line on the lower edge. The small trim piece on the lower back is cut of striped silk, finished on the edges, gathered down the broken line to fit across the centre-back piece at the mark, and stitched down on the same line.

At each **X** a short tie of striped silk lined with brown silk satin – 20 x 1.2cm (8 x ½in) – is topstitched. The one on the right side ends with a self-fabric button, and the other holds a buttonhole. These meet in front in order to hold the front of the spencer to the body.

The curved (and lined) sleeves are very typical of late eighteenth century dress. They are represented in the pattern with a single shape; the plain line at the sleeve head is the upper piece, and the broken line the lower one. The sleeves are open to the mark on the outer seam, where the lining is whipped to the striped silk. The back sleeve is pieced on the broken lines, with the stripes matching perfectly, and has brown silk death's head buttons where marked. The front sleeve holds brown silk thread eyes on the edge of the opening to match.

Right: *Detail of the wrist of the heavy silk spencer, courtesy of Old Sturbridge Village, Sturbridge, MA (26.8.10).*

Right: *Named after George Spencer, 2nd Earl Spencer, the tailless coat was adopted by ladies of the 1790s who wore it as we might wear a cardigan. The spencer was tailored to match the lines of the dress worn underneath.*

Regency Women's Dress

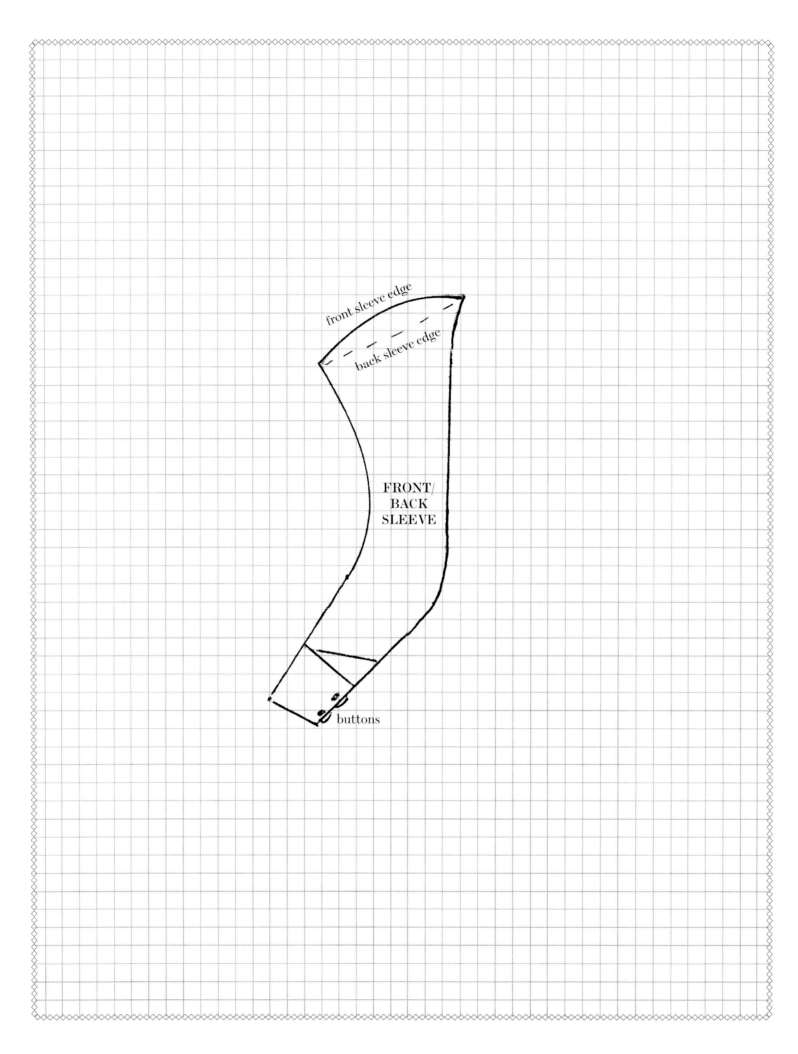

front sleeve edge

back sleeve edge

FRONT/
BACK
SLEEVE

buttons

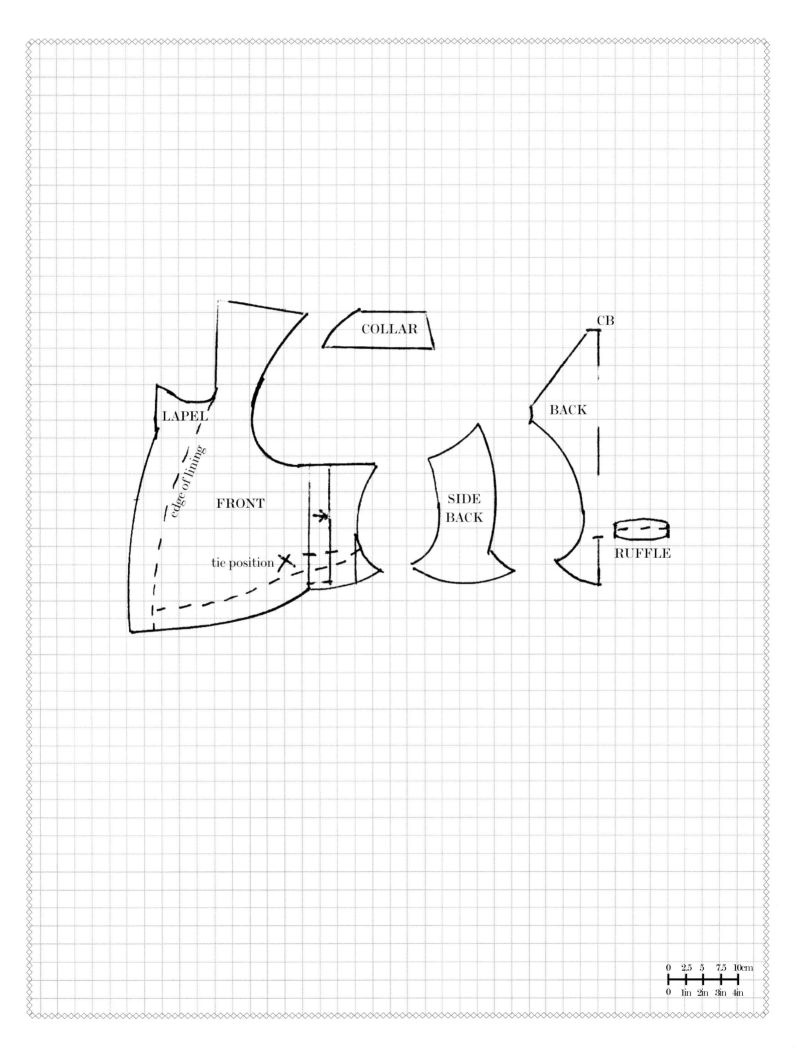

COLLAR

CB

LAPEL

BACK

edge of lining

FRONT

SIDE
BACK

tie position ✕

RUFFLE

0  2.5  5  7.5  10cm

0  1in  2in  3in  4in

# Spencer
## 1810–1813

This spencer was likely not intended for serious winter wear: although the body is padded with cotton or wool for extra warmth, there is no trace of any sort of fastening to hold the front closed. The outer layer is a lavender silk taffeta; the lining is a lighter taffeta in off-white.

The lining appears to have been made up first, the pieces lapped and topstitched in the same way as the lavender taffeta; the body was then padded and covered with the exterior fabric. The front piece is lapped over the side under the arm, the side piece lapping the back at the curved side-back seam, and the front lapping the back at the shoulder seam. The internal seams are sewn with an off-white thread, while the visible seams are sewn in lavender. The front is darted through all layers and backstitched inside, the darts turned towards the centre front. The lower edge is faced with a lavender piping, the upper edge of which is sewn through all layers with a miniscule spaced backstitch. The front edges are also piped, but the piping runs between the layers.

The collar, made of two layers of lavender taffeta and piped around the edges, is sewn to the body around the neckline; the seam allowances are covered with a bias strip of whiter silk.

The short oversleeves and long undersleeves are sewn into the armholes together. The oversleeves are unlined and the slits are bound with lavender taffeta, the lower edge faced with piping; the leaf shapes are backed with a cotton bobbinet, piped, and pleated at the bottom, then tucked into the slits and sewn into place. The undersleeve lining and exterior fabric are sewn separately, and the wrist edge is faced with a bias strip of lavender taffeta.

Left: *Sleeve detail of summer spencer, courtesy of Old Sturbridge Village, Sturbridge, MA (26.8.8).*

Right: *Morning dress, c.1810. A white muslin dress with a high stand collar and single ruff is worn with a pale green spencer with collar and lapels.*

gathered to 20cm (8in)

OVERSLEEVE

gathered to 23cm (9in)

CB

FRONT

SIDE
BACK

BACK

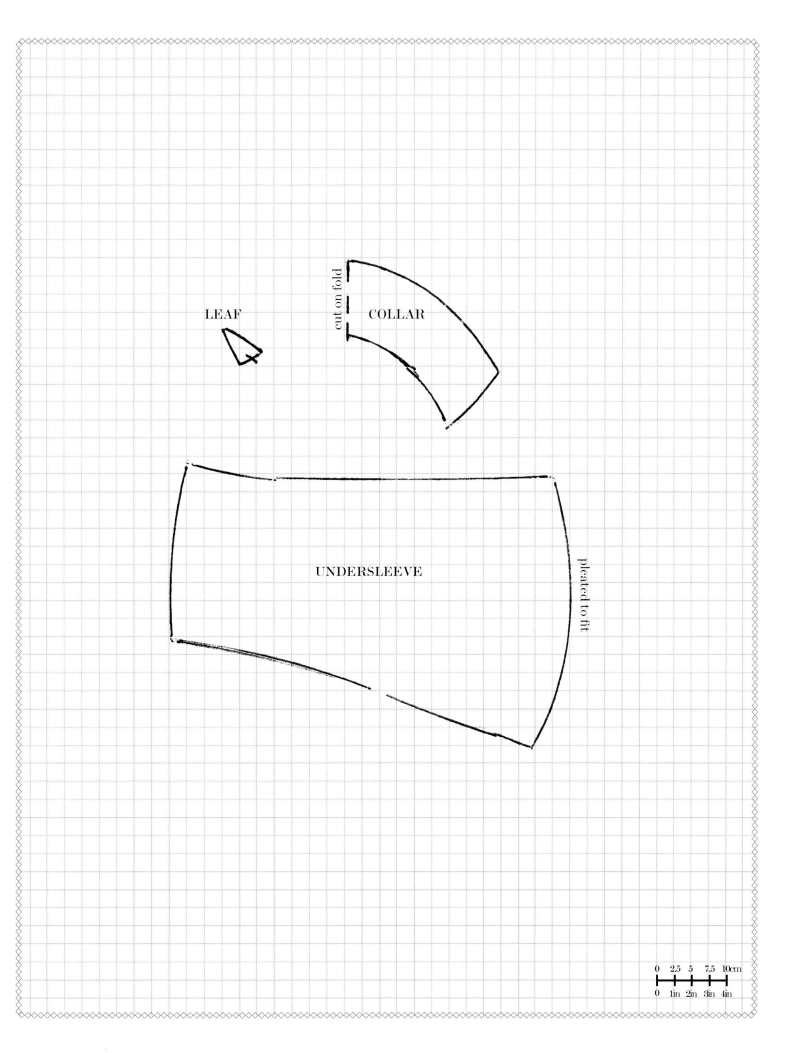

LEAF

COLLAR

cut on fold

UNDERSLEEVE

pleated to fit

0   2.5   5   7.5   10cm

0   1in  2in  3in  4in

# Morning Dress
## 1795–1803 (fabric c.1785)

This cotton-print chemise gown (lined with linen) has been said to be a maternity gown, but the construction is typical of ordinary dress for women during the transitional period, developed from the chemise gowns of the 1780s.

The centre-back seam is sewn in the lining and cotton together with no attempt at matching the pattern, the seam allowances turned towards the wearer and whipped down with black thread. After this, the rest of the lining is sewn together with the seam allowances away from the wearer; the front of the lining is pieced as shown on the pattern. The cotton pieces are then topstitched on top, the side pieces over the back, the front pieces over the sides, and the straps over the fronts and backs. The fronts are pleated under the arm as shown on the pattern, and stitched down to the lining on the broken lines. The neckline in the printed cotton houses a drawstring; there is no shaping or closure for the waist in front. The centre front is open down to the first mark, and is sewn together from the first to the second marks. The neckline in the linen layer is hemmed.

The gown originally had two ties, which were sewn into the side seams; one remains, no longer attached. These would have held the gown closed at the waist, and fitted it to the body.

The sleeves, flatlined in linen, are pieced as shown in the cotton layer and are open from the mark down to the wrist. While their shape is highly reminiscent of eighteenth-century sleeves, they are not set in in the eighteenth-century manner, but are backstitched into the armhole all the way around.

The back of the skirt is in two wide panels, slightly shaped at top and bottom, and the whole is backstitched to the bodice. The hem is 6cm (2½in) deep at the front and 11.5cm (4½in) deep at the back.

Left: *Detail of fabric from the floral morning dress, courtesy of the New York State Historical Association, Cooperstown, NY (N255-1953).*

Right: *Detail from* Cinderella By The Fireside *by Henry Richter (c.1795). Morning dress tended to be plain or made from recycled fabrics as they were worn indoors.*

Regency Women's Dress

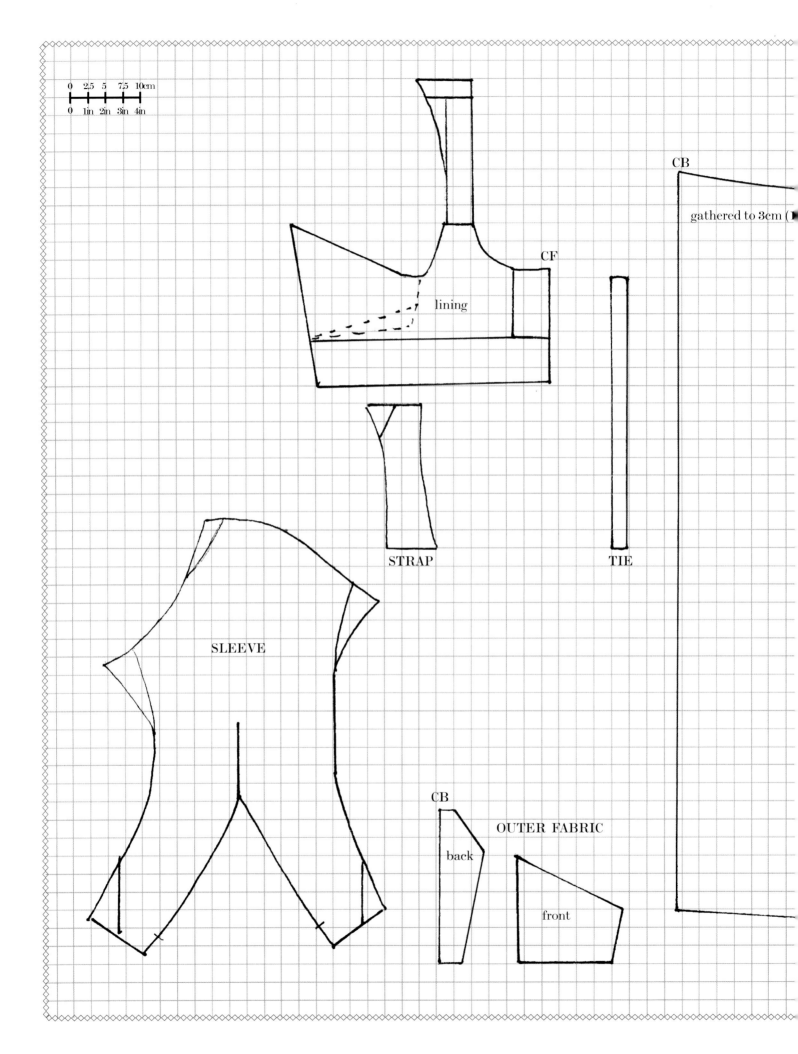

0  2.5  5  7.5  10cm

0  1in  2in  3in  4in

CF

lining

CB

gathered to 3cm (▶

STRAP

TIE

SLEEVE

CB

OUTER FABRIC

back

front

0  2.5  5  7.5  10cm

0  1in  2in  3in  4in

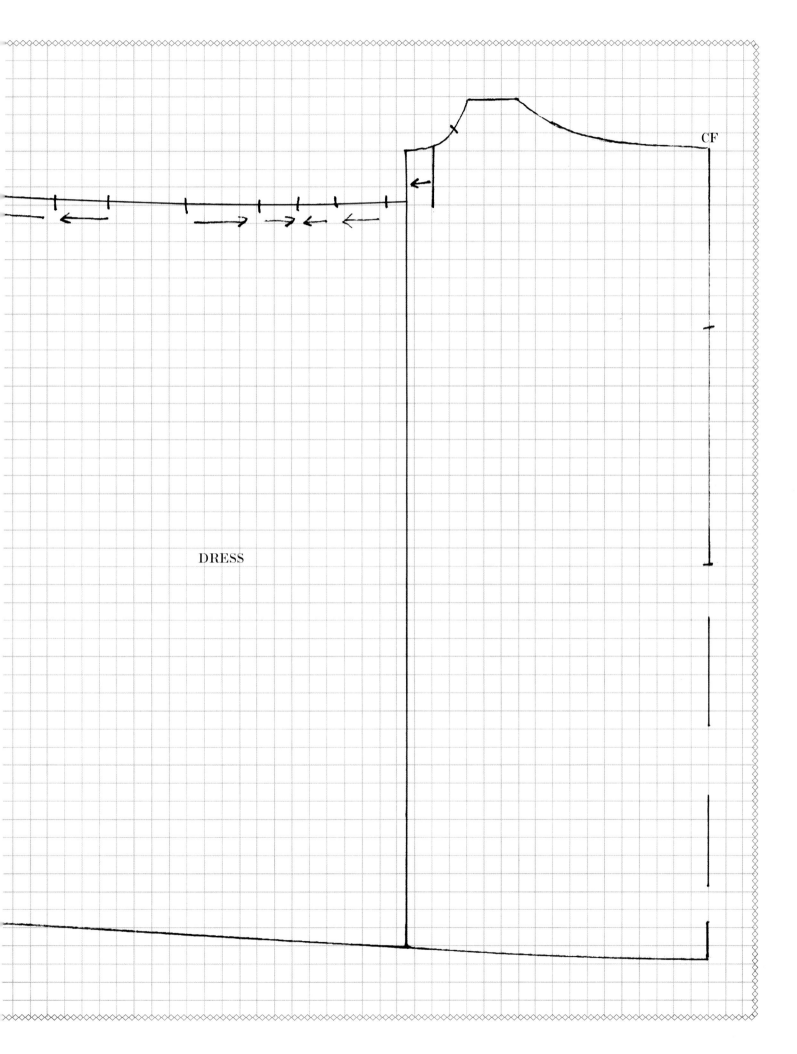

DRESS

CF

# Morning or Evening Dress

## 1803–1806

This unlined white cotton dress is embroidered heavily in white cotton thread. The front piece of the bodice is embroidered with the narrower motif patterned above the sleeve at ¼ scale, and with three leafy motifs: the solid leaves are satin-stitched, while the outlined ones are cut and filled with knit lace and edged with satin stitch. The upper edge has a pair of eyelets (marked) in the hem, which holds a very narrow cord to pull in the neckline; the lower edge is mostly gathered near the sides. On the side edges, the piece is narrowly pleated three times between the marks to 4cm (1½in).

The strap is overlapped by the front piece, the outer edge of the strap running along the outer edge of the front; it emerges from behind the piece at the marks

and runs over the shoulder to the back, where it is lapped by the side-back piece. The side piece laps the edge of the front piece and is topstitched through all layers; it also laps and is topstitched to the side-back piece. This seam, as well as the seam to the strap, is covered with a double row of French knots. The side-back piece is folded down on the drawn seamline and sewn to the centre-back piece on the broken line to give it the look of a tuck. The bottom edges of the front and side pieces are turned to the inside and whipped to the waistband, while the side-back piece is slightly longer than them and has a band the same width added to the inside. The centre-back piece has a short waistband segment topstitched at the upper edge to the bodice piece. The back neckline holds a 3mm (⅛in) tape to fasten the gown.

The side edges of the sleeves are slightly pleated at the bottom before seaming. The lower edge is trimmed with the edging embroidery; the large motif is embroidered on the bias at the corner of the sleeve, flanked on either side with the motif from the centre of the bodice front.

The skirt pieces are patterned to the bottom of the waistband: they extend another 12mm (½in) upwards behind the waistband and form the back of a channel which holds a second tape. The bottom edge of the waistband is topstitched to the skirt. The front of the skirt is sewn flat to the waistband to the mark, and is pleated to 2cm (¾in) from the mark to the seam, the pleats pointing towards the back. The back skirt piece was cut down to the second mark and seamed back up to the first, where it is open. The lower edge of the skirt is embroidered first with the narrow edging, then with the large motifs. The large motifs also border the sides of the front skirt piece.

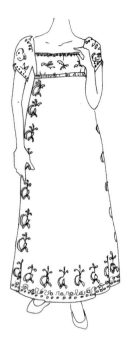

Left: *White embroidered dress courtesy of the Brookside Museum and Saratoga County Historical Society, Ballston Spa, NY (1981.25.2). This detail shows the embellishment on the sleeve.*

Right: *Evening dresses featured in* Lady's Magazine, *October 1803. A yellow gown with round neckline is worn with matching turban and slippers, while a light blue gown and white tunic shows how this pattern might be adapted with a divided front cut away at the sides.*

Regency Women's Dress

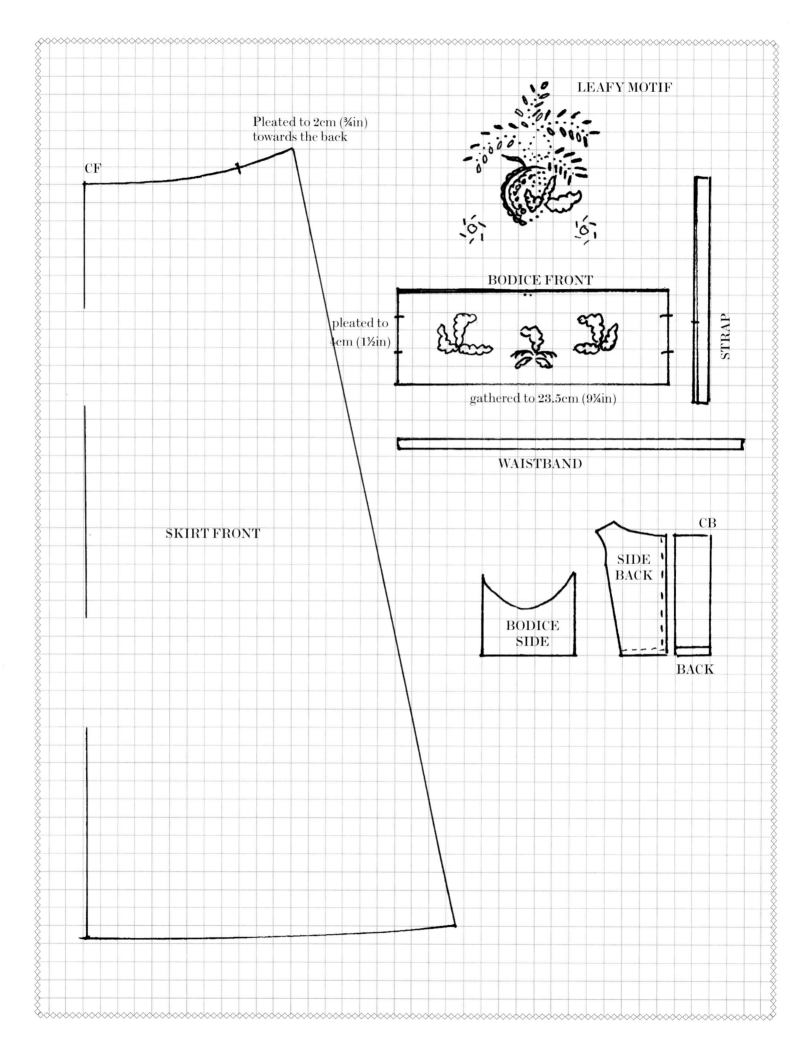

LEAFY MOTIF

CF

Pleated to 2cm (¾in)
towards the back

pleated to
4cm (1½in)

SKIRT FRONT

BODICE FRONT

gathered to 23.5cm (9¼in)

WAISTBAND

STRAP

CB

SIDE
BACK

BODICE
SIDE

BACK

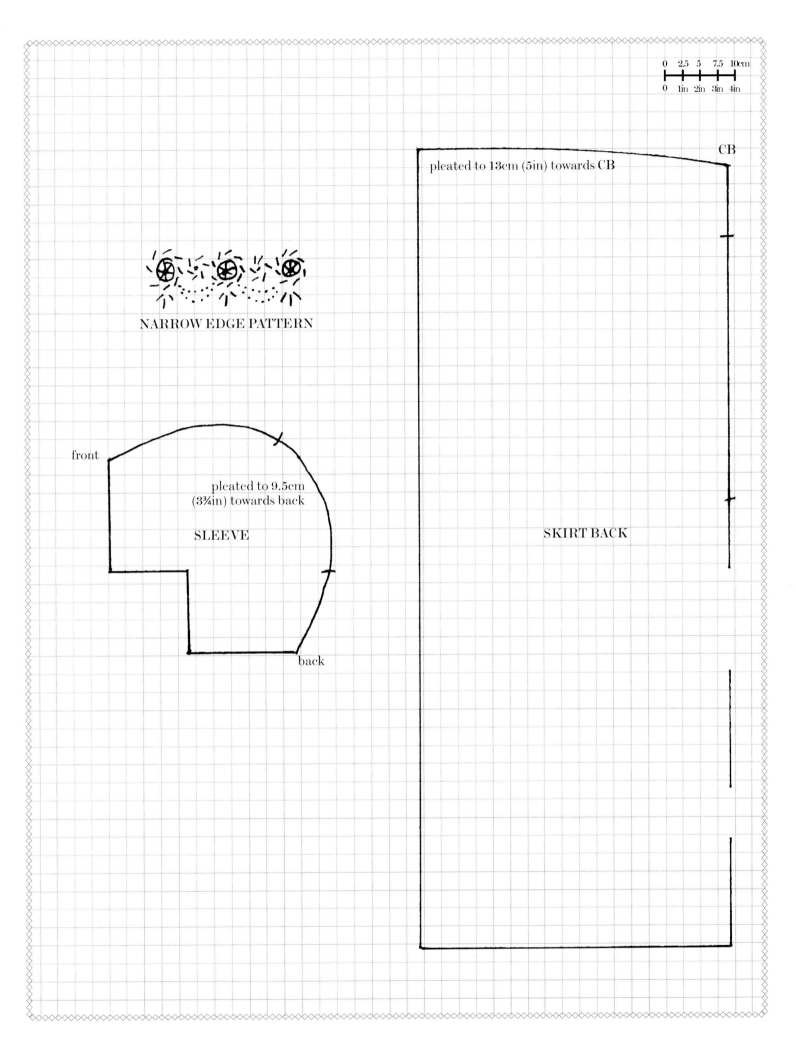

NARROW EDGE PATTERN

front

pleated to 9.5cm
(3¾in) towards back

SLEEVE

back

pleated to 13cm (5in) towards CB

CB

SKIRT BACK

0   2.5   5   7.5   10cm

0   1in   2in   3in   4in

# Morning Dress
## c.1800

The turn of the century was a transitional period of great experimentation in women's dressmaking, as the construction techniques that had been used with only minor alterations for most of the eighteenth century were not as suited to the lighter materials and less-structured shapes of the high-waisted styles. These techniques had never been well-suited to gowns with closed skirts, either, so solutions had been worked out to achieve that look: the 'bib front' dress grew out of the apron front, seen in the Quaker gown (see page 66) and in other dresses through the 1780s and early 1790s. The bib-front style appears to be specific to England. This gown was said to have been brought from Scotland by a Marguerite Allen in 1800.

The bodice is lined in linen; the gown is a white cotton printed in black and tan. The lining extends beyond the cotton to form the flaps in front, which are covered by the bib when worn; both the lining and cotton extend down to the broken lines in the bodice, while the skirt is sewn to the plain line. The only seams in the bodice are sewn in a running whipstitch through all layers, with the seam allowances turned between them. The sleeves, also lined, are backstitched into the bodice. White thread bars are made between the marks on the side-back seams in order to hold skirt ties, which no longer exist. White yarn is whipped across the inside of the centre-back bodice piece, to tie in front (under the bib) and hold the back of the gown to the wearer.

The skirt is made with an extremely long, squared train. The centre-back panel has one seam in it, down the right side (shown on the pattern); it and the side panel, which is cut upside down on the fabric, are pleated as shown and backstitched to the bodice. The front panel is sewn to the side panel only up to the bottom of the placket, which is topstitched to the panel, and the top edge is hemmed widely enough to include a self-fabric drawstring. The bib is whipped flat to the front of the skirt between the marks, with the hem on the top edge holding two eyelets in order to allow the neckline to be tightened.

Left: *Elegant morning dress courtesy of the New York State Historical Association, Cooperstown, NY (N138-52). This detail shows the back waist.*

Right: *A French engraving of c.1903 shows the sporting fashions of the era, where a group of ladies enjoy a spell outdoors. Their gowns have half-length sleeves and low, square necklines.*

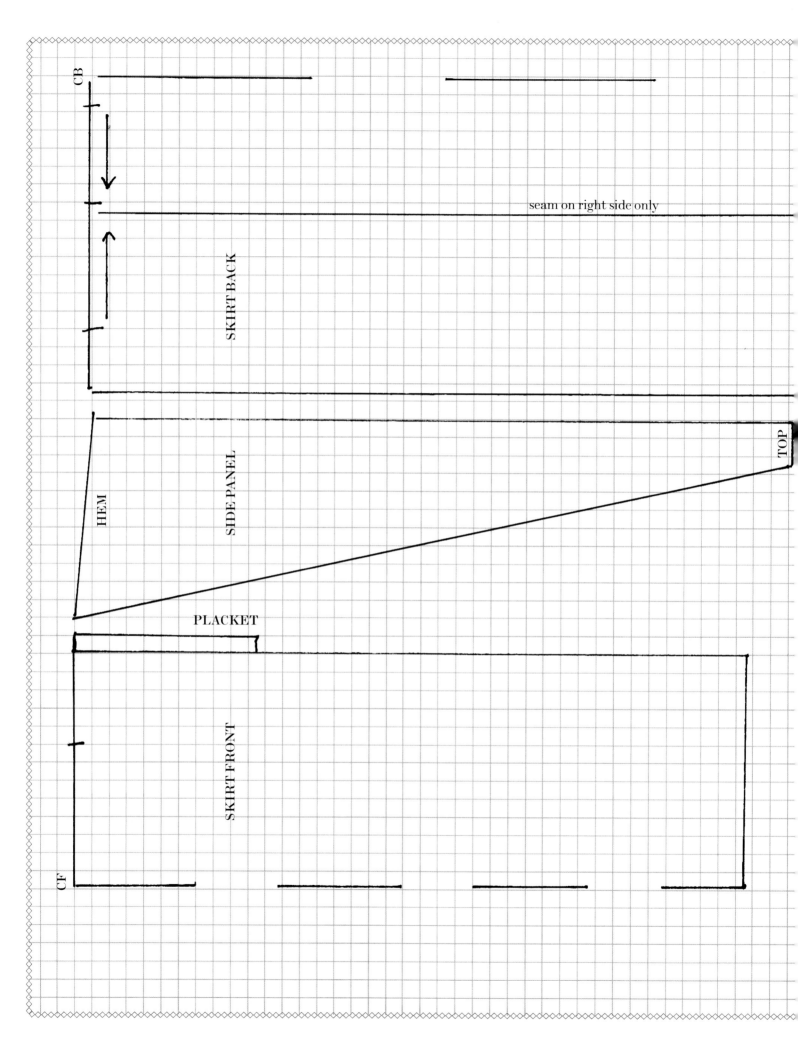

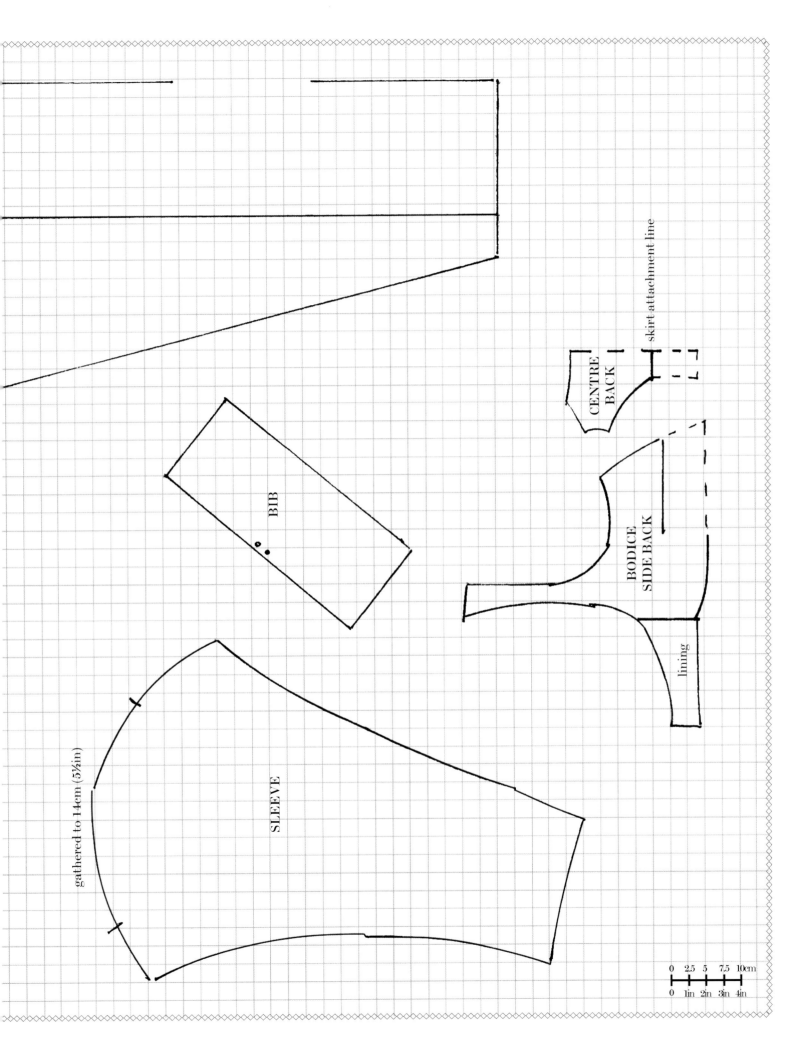

BIB

SLEEVE

gathered to 14cm (5½in)

CENTRE BACK

skirt attachment line

BODICE SIDE BACK

lining

0  2.5  5  7.5  10cm

0  1in  2in  3in  4in

# Morning Dress
## 1800–1805

This bib-front dress (likely of British origin, though the exact provenance is unknown) is cut without a train. It is accessorized with removable undersleeves and a removable chemisette, both of the same cotton print as the gown. Adding them would have made the gown more suitable for cold weather, while wearing the gown without them would make it cooler in the summer heat.

The construction of the bodice is very similar to that of the previous gown. In this case, the lining was made up first and the front pieces topstitched over the back at the side-back seams, while the straps, hemmed on the neckline edge, are sandwiched between the layers and the back is topstitched over them. The loops on the side-back seams are of the same cotton print. The short upper sleeve (the cotton cut on the bias, the lining on the grain) is set into the armhole, while the long sleeves

are currently not attached: they would have been tacked (basted) into the upper sleeve. They are made up flat, and are open from the top to the marks.

The skirt is pleated, gathered, and gauged as shown on the pattern, and the top of the skirt panel is hemmed and sewn to the waistband; the lower edge of the bib is turned in, and the bib is whipped to the waistband as well. The top edge of the bib is hemmed and very slightly gathered, possibly on a tape enclosed in the hem. The waistband ends run through loops on the back of the bodice and tie.

The simple chemisette is of the same printed cotton, made of slightly shaped rectangles and with a collar 9cm (3½in) high. There is no fastening: it would have been tucked under the neckline to stay in place.

Left: *Morning dress courtesy of Old Sturbridge Village, Sturbridge, MA (26.33.166a-d). This detail shows the inside back of the garment.*

Right: French print c.1802 of ladies playing hide and seek in a garden.

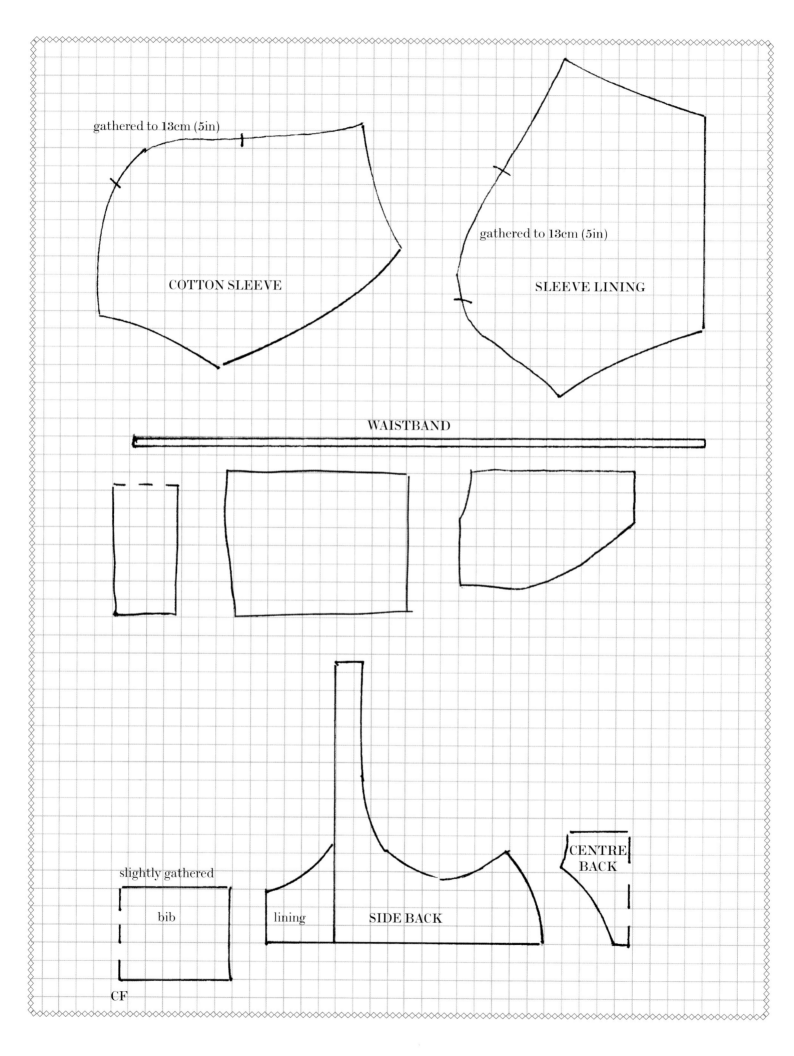

gathered to 13cm (5in)

COTTON SLEEVE

gathered to 13cm (5in)

SLEEVE LINING

WAISTBAND

slightly gathered

bib

CF

lining

SIDE BACK

CENTRE
BACK

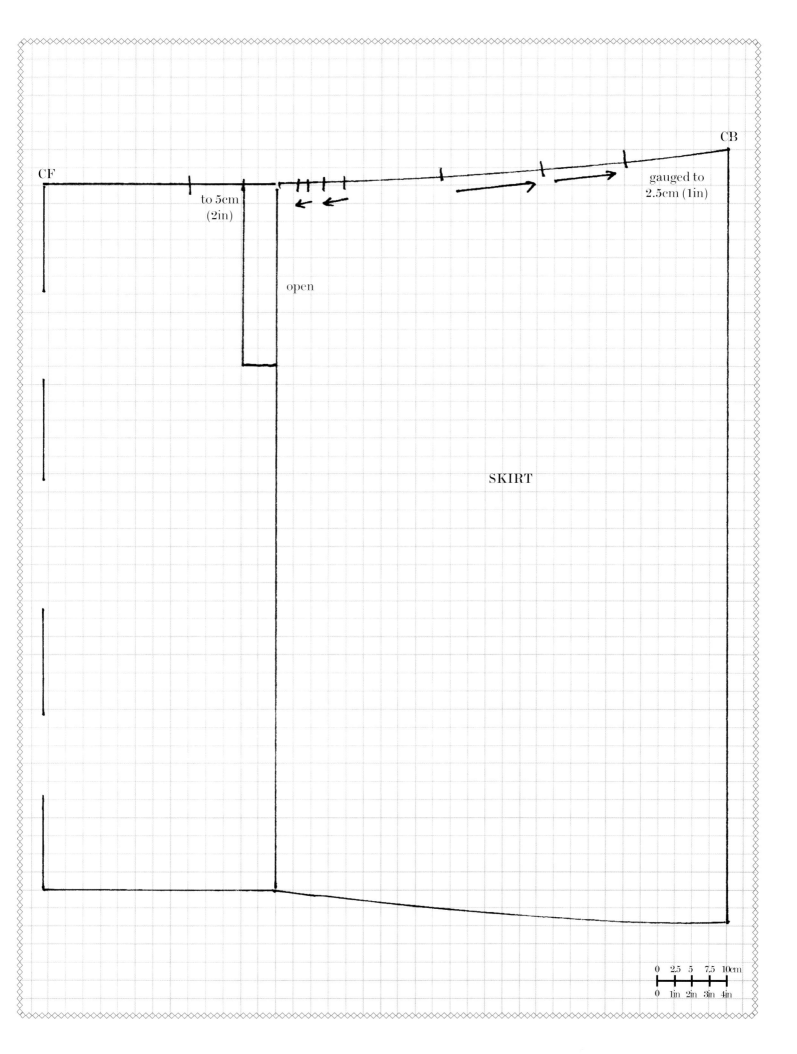

CB

CF

to 5cm
(2in)

open

gauged to
2.5cm (1in)

SKIRT

0   2.5   5   7.5   10cm

0   1in  2in  3in  4in

# Morning or Evening Dress

## 1803–1805

This gown is said to have been worn by Parthena Ann Lake, who married Asa Spafford (both of Westerlo, New York) on January 1, 1817. It is more likely that it was made for someone of her mother's generation, as it is too early for her to have worn it and would have been unfashionable by the time of her young adulthood.

The front and back of the bodice are mostly unlined green silk taffeta, while the side piece is flatlined with cotton; the front and back are flatlined from the seams to the vertical broken lines. The front neckline and waist are hemmed and gathered over cords, which are completely sewn into the gown, rather than being adjustable by the wearer. The back neckline and waist also hold cords which gather the taffeta, and tie at the centre back to fasten the gown. The flatlined sleeves are backstitched into the armholes.

The front panel of the skirt is sewn flat to the bodice, gathering slightly at the sides. The vertical seam to the side of the back is only on the right side. The hem of the skirt appears to have been let down 4cm (1½in). Originally, it would have had a simple hem, but after it was let down the skirt was faced with an 11cm (4½in) wide band of black wool.

Left: *Back of the green silk gown. Gown courtesy of the New York State Historical Association, Cooperstown, NY (N401-1950).*

Right: *A young woman in a high-waisted, classical style, wearing a white muslin gown with the simple, square-necked dresses of the early 1800s. Miniature by Friedrich Karl Groeger (1807).*

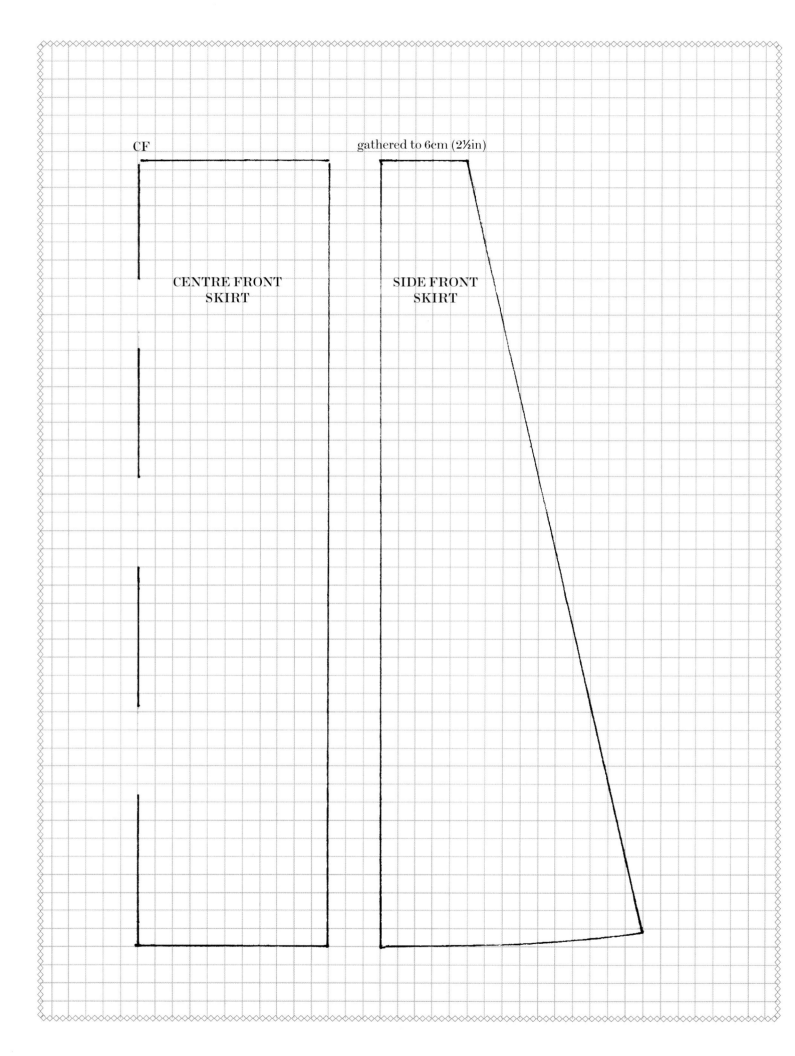

CF

gathered to 6cm (2½in)

CENTRE FRONT
SKIRT

SIDE FRONT
SKIRT

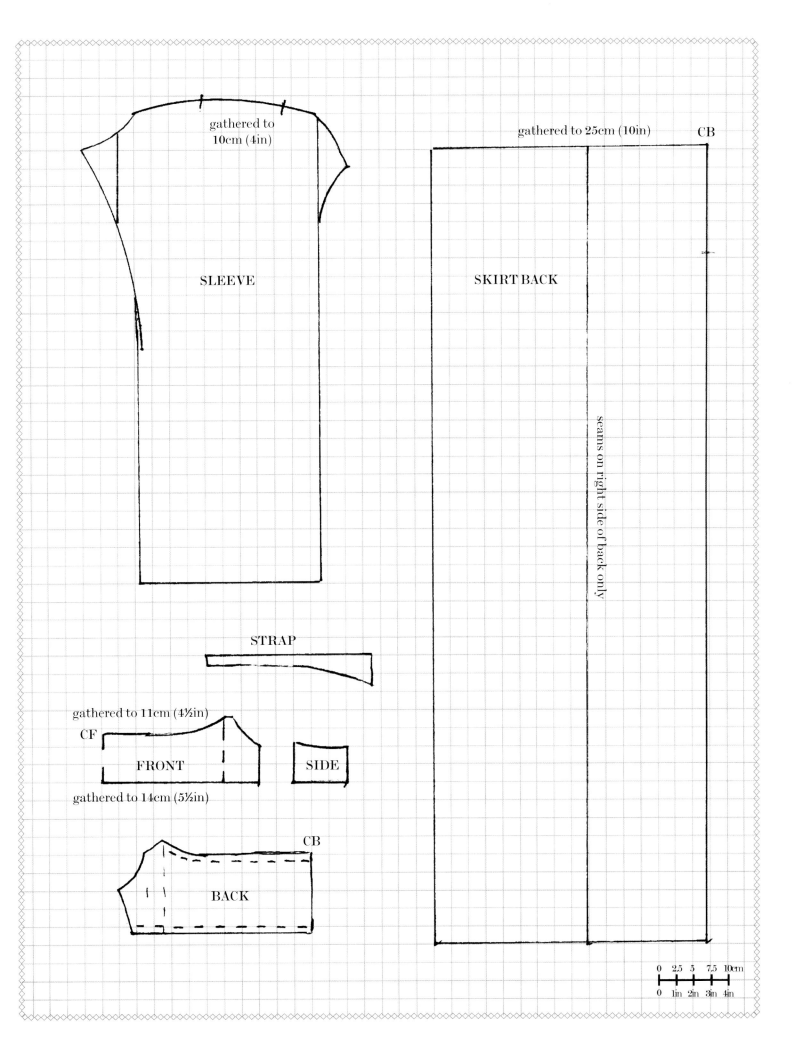

gathered to
10cm (4in)

SLEEVE

gathered to 25cm (10in)                    CB

SKIRT BACK

seams on right side of back only

STRAP

gathered to 11cm (4½in)

CF

FRONT                    SIDE

gathered to 14cm (5½in)

CB

BACK

0   2.5   5   7.5  10cm

0   1in  2in  3in  4in

# Evening Dress
## 1804–1810

This gown of robin's-egg blue silk taffeta is largely unlined, with the side piece flatlined in white cotton and the back flatlined to the broken line; the silk of the side piece is pieced independently of the lining. The front of the bodice is darted slightly, with the darts turned towards the centre and topstitched. The inside of the neckline hem holds an eyelet 12mm (½in) from the centre on either side, in order to allow the neckline to be slightly gathered to fit. The unlined strap attaches to the front from the mark to the edge of the piece. The back silk and lining lap the side piece and are topstitched down. The back neckline and waist are both gathered on drawstrings: the neckline drawstring is a narrow, yellowed white silk ribbon, while the waist drawstring is a wide but lightweight light green silk ribbon.

The puffed sleeve is heavily pieced in vertical strips. The lower edge of the sleeve is whipped to the outer side of the binding; the binding is then turned in and whipped down.

The skirt attachment to the bodice front was altered during the period. The bottom of the bodice is currently turned up and to the inside over a folded linen tape, with the skirt lapped over it and topstitched down. The rest of the skirt is backstitched to the bodice as usual. The bottom of the skirt itself is tucked as shown; the left side of the front is then tucked with the tuck pointing toward the centre front; the right side of the front, because it doesn't have the tuck, is only 34cm (13½in) wide.

Left: *Blue silk dress courtesy of the New York State Historical Association, Cooperstown, NY (N1358-1943), showing a detail of the back.*

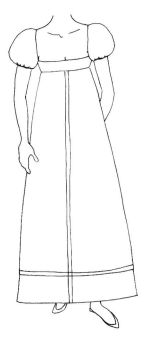

Right: Modes for 1809,
*a fashion illustration by*
*H de Viel Castel, showing*
*a gown with vandyked and*
*embroidered hem.*

Regency Women's Dress

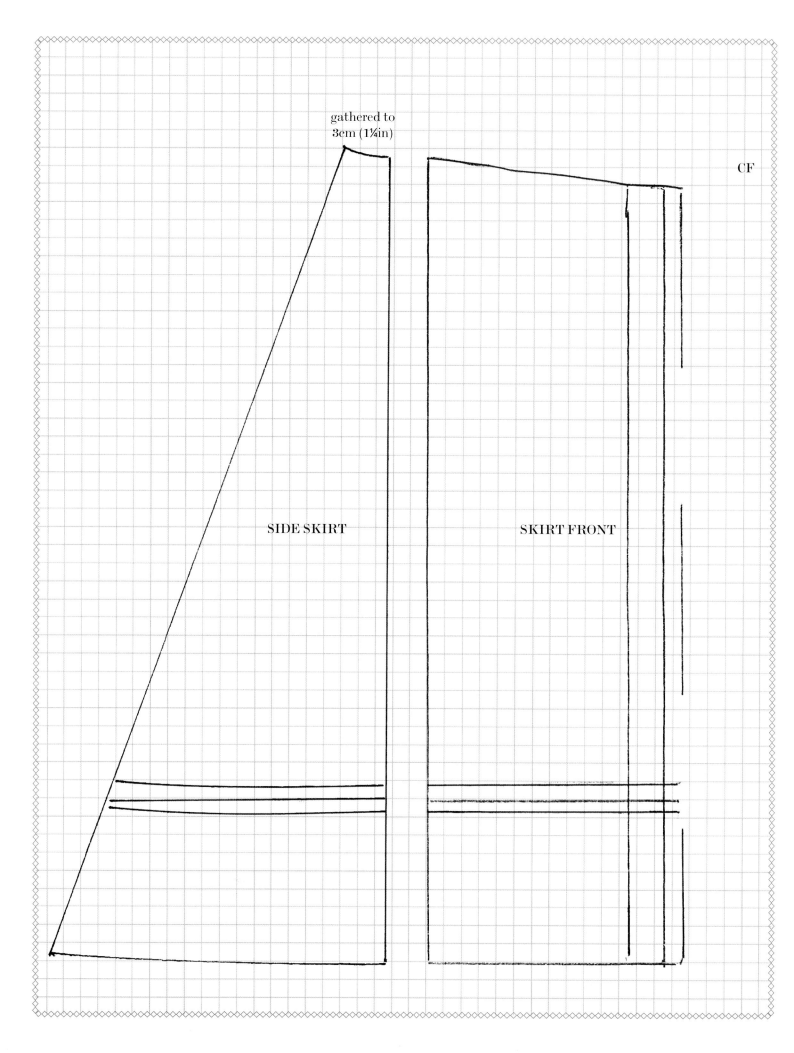

gathered to
3cm (1¼in)

SIDE SKIRT

SKIRT FRONT

CF

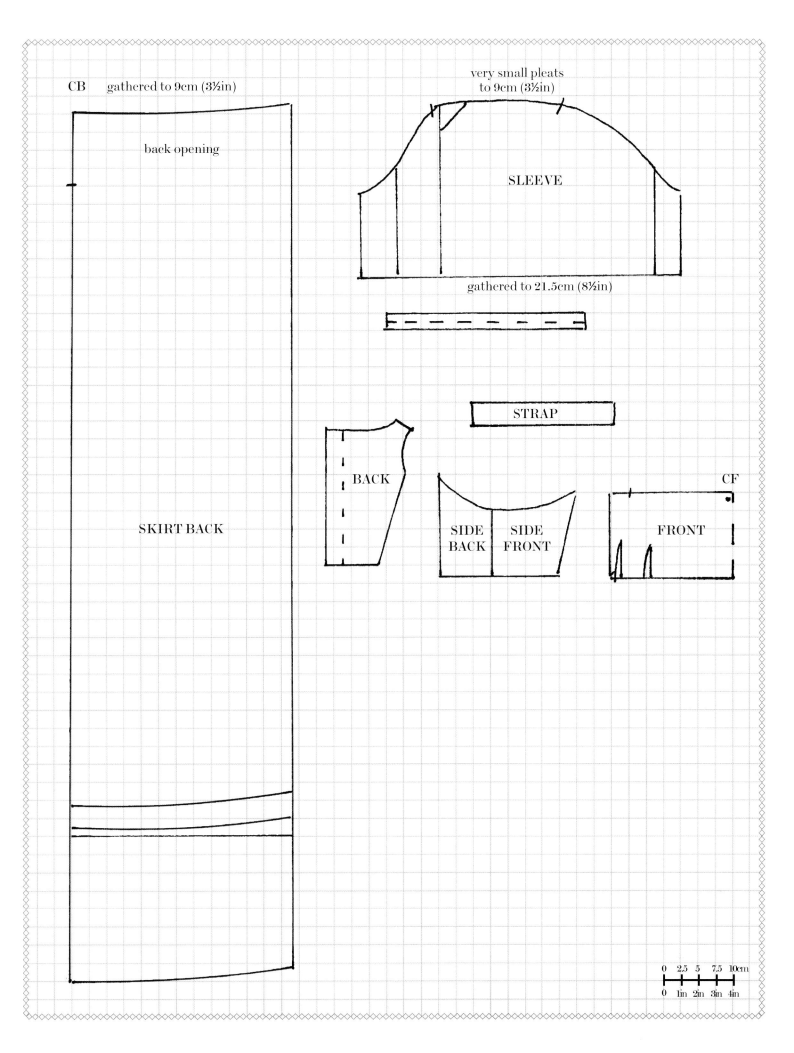

CB    gathered to 9cm (3½in)

back opening

very small pleats
to 9cm (3½in)

SLEEVE

gathered to 21.5cm (8½in)

STRAP

SKIRT BACK

BACK

SIDE
BACK

SIDE
FRONT

CF

FRONT

CB    gathered to 9cm (3½in)

0    2.5    5    7.5    10cm

0    1in    2in    3in    4in

# Evening Dress
## 1805–1808

This gown, made of a white cotton mull embroidered on the bolt with white leaf motifs, is said to have been owned by Margaretta Sanders (1764–1830), wife of the prominent Kiliaen Van Rensselaer (1763–1845, married in 1791). It is highly unusual in that it has neither a front opening nor a back one: instead, the mull fabric of the front is sewn on either side to short side pieces with straps, while the left side piece is not sewn to anything on its left side and the lining beneath (to which it is not sewn) is not attached to the skirt. This allows the weight of the skirt to hold the strap to the shoulder when the dress is worn, but also allows the wearer to simply pull off the dress rather than have to unfasten it in the back.

The front-opening linen lining of the bodice was constructed first. The fronts are darted, with the darts turned toward the centre and sewn down on both sides; the back lining piece extends down to the broken lines. The cotton pieces are then layered on, the side pieces lapped and topstitched over the back, the right strap lapped over the side piece, and the left understrap (the section of the left front lining from the left side to the vertical line) lapped over the left side and stitched down to the lining. Both the left and right cotton strap pieces are lapped and topstitched over the rectangular front piece. The lower edge of the front is slightly gathered at either side, while the upper edge has a pair of eyelets in the centre front of the neckline hem in order to allow the neckline to be tightened on a pair of ribbons or cords.

A belt of cotton mull, 77.5cm (30½in) long and 1.5cm ($^5/_8$in) wide when folded in half down the length, is attached to the back piece across the bottom of the bodice. Two self-fabric buttons are placed where marked at the side-back seams; the belt is sewn down

with them. This belt ties in the front, helping to hold the gown closed down the side opening.

The sleeves are unlined and backstitched into the armhole – on the left side, they are only sewn to the lined sections. The bottom of the sleeve is gathered on the broken line and whipped to a 2mm ($^1/_8$in) wide linen tape to create a ruffled edge.

The right-front side seam of the skirt is open at the placket, which is cut of a piece on the straight of grain; the top and bottom edges of this placket are sewn over the side panel. On the left side, the seam is open down to the level of the bottom of the placket. The front and side panel pieces of the skirt are topstitched flat to the bodice, as well as the back panel (seamed where shown only on the right side) to the mark. On the left side of the skirt, the side panel and the flat part of the back panel are sewn on the dotted line to the bodice. The skirt is tucked as shown near the lower edge, and the hem is 3cm (1¼in) deep.

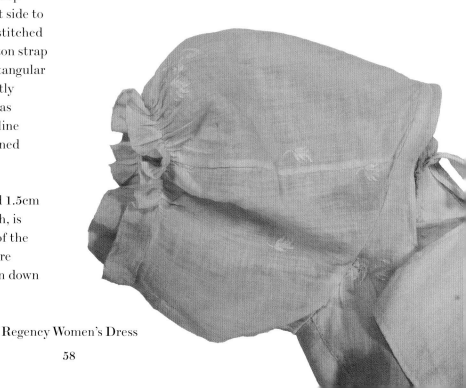

Left: *Detail of sleeve, from the embroidered white gown courtesy of the Albany Institute of History and Art, Albany, NY (U1973.83).*

Right: *Fashion plate for Costume Parisien (1805) of a white gown with self-embroidered hem and white scarf worn like braces.*

Regency Women's Dress

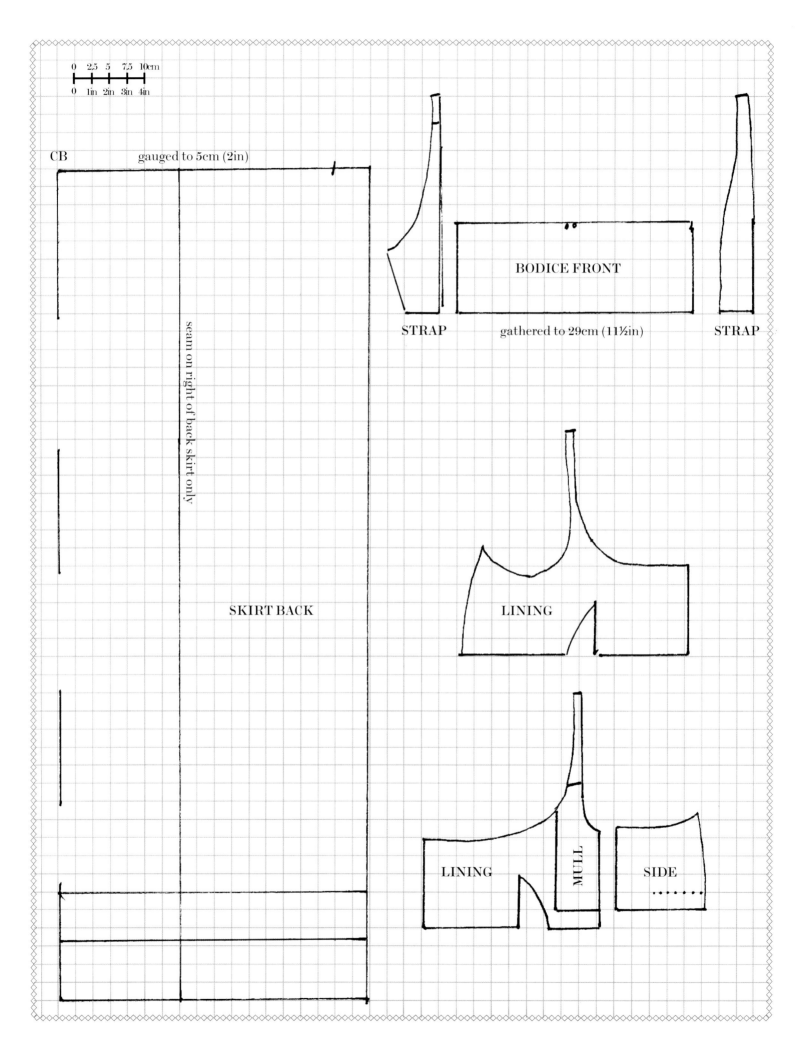

0 2.5 5 7.5 10cm

0 1in 2in 3in 4in

CB       gauged to 5cm (2in)

seam on right of back skirt only

SKIRT BACK

STRAP

BODICE FRONT

gathered to 29cm (11½in)

STRAP

LINING

LINING

MULL

SIDE

0 2.5 5 7.5 10cm

0 1in 2in 3in 4in

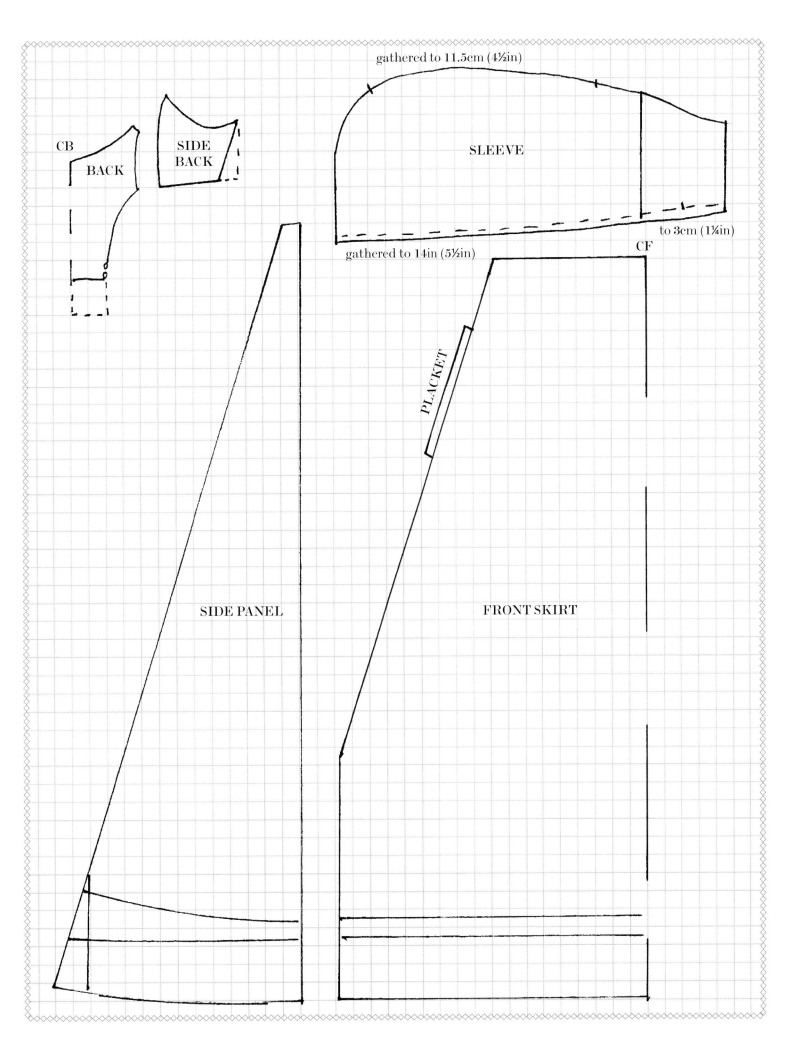

CB

BACK

SIDE
BACK

gathered to 11.5cm (4½in)

SLEEVE

to 3cm (1¼in)

gathered to 14in (5½in)

CF

PLACKET

SIDE PANEL

FRONT SKIRT

# Morning Dress
## 1809–1818

The closely woven white cotton of this dress is called percale (*perkale*, in the French fashion press). It was very commonly used for the plain white dresses so emblematic of the era, as well as lightweight summer hats and bonnets. Evening dresses were short sleeved so this is a morning dress.

The entire gown is unlined. The side and back pieces are seamed with 2mm (¹/₈in) piping, while the front is lapped over the sides and topstitched. The top of the sleeve is set into the armhole so that the back of the gusset is in line with the side seam. Above the wrist,

which is trimmed with a very narrow scalloped net, the sleeve is sewn in ten pintucks. The neckline, shoulder seam and armhole are also piped.

The skirt is topstitched to the bodice across the front to the marks and backstitched to the bodice and a 2mm (¹/₈in) tape where it is gathered. While the back neckline has no fastening at all, there is a metal hook and eye sewn to the waistline at centre back.

The lower edge of the skirt is cut in large scallops which are themselves cut in tiny scallops, about 6mm (¼in) wide, each holding an eyelet. Inside the large scallop is an embroidered floral motif including a carnation, a leaf, and a bud with bobbinet insertion. Bobbinet is a type of tulle netting made by machines which were invented by John Heathcoat in 1808. He set up his factory in Nottingham, but after it was attacked by Luddites afraid of the new technology, he moved to Devon. The inclusion of bobbinet lace helps date this dress.

Left: *Detail of hem, from embroidered cotton dress courtesy of the New York State Museum, Albany, NY (2007.63.64).*

Regency Women's Dress

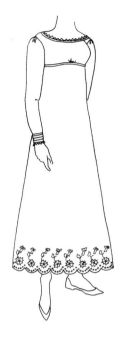

Right: *Fashion plate (1816)*
*showing a white percale dress.*
*Like our dress, it features*
*tucks and hem detailing.*

Regency Women's Dress

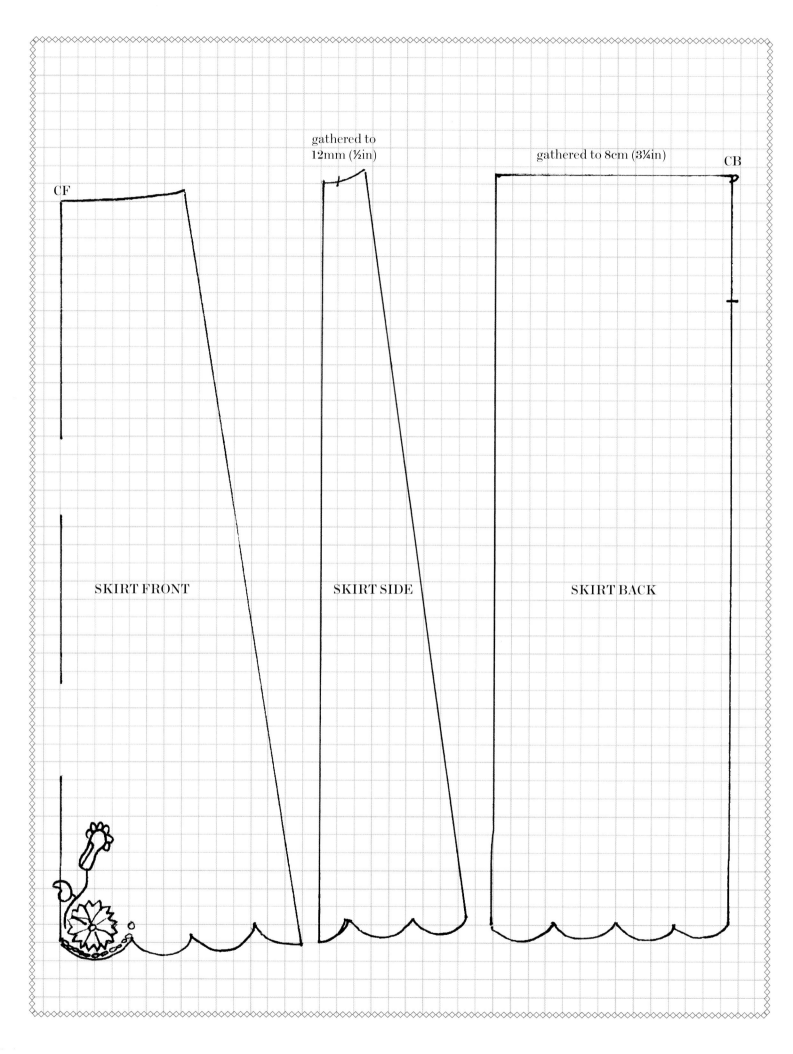

CF

gathered to
12mm (½in)

gathered to 8cm (3¼in)

CB

SKIRT FRONT

SKIRT SIDE

SKIRT BACK

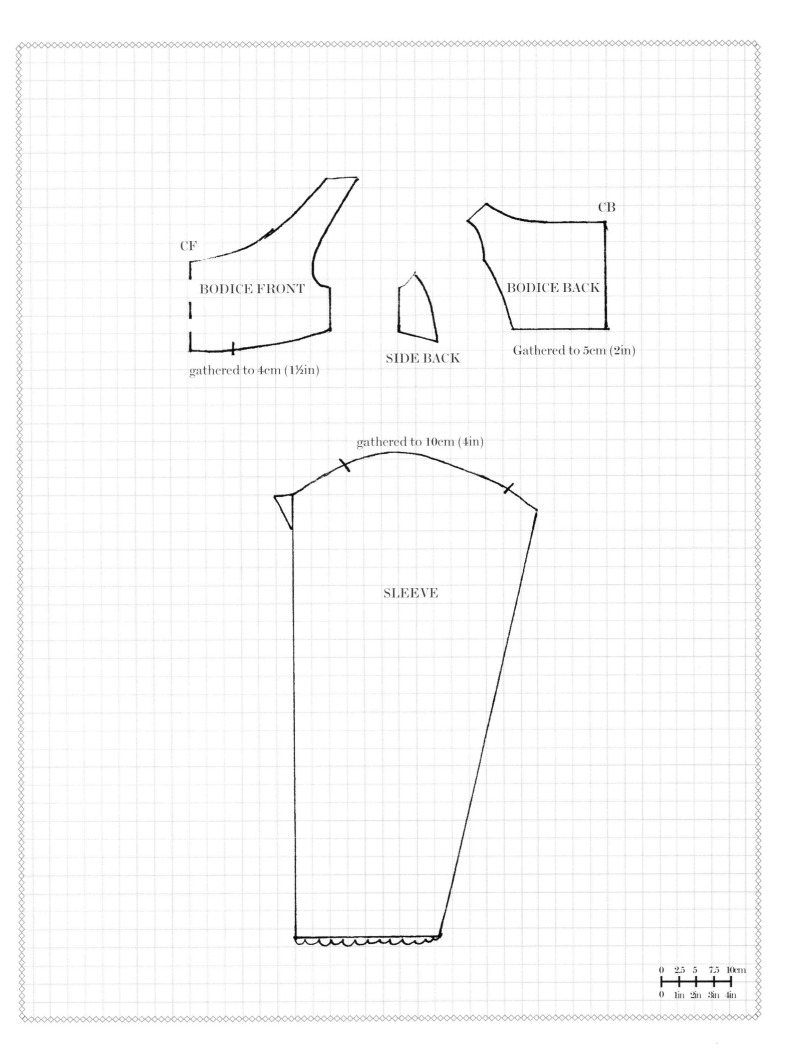

CF

BODICE FRONT

gathered to 4cm (1½in)

SIDE BACK

CB

BODICE BACK

Gathered to 5cm (2in)

gathered to 10cm (4in)

SLEEVE

0   2.5   5   7.5   10cm

0   1in   2in   3in   4in

# Quaker Gown
## 1810–1820

The cut of this dark green silk gown is extraordinarily reminiscent of another in the Museum of Fine Arts Boston (52.1769), as well as one in the New Bedford Whaling Museum (1991.45.5). Like those, this one is probably also a Quaker woman's garment: the apron-fronted skirt appears to have been a very common construction for 'plain dress'.

The bodice of the gown is lined in a light tan cotton. The lining was sewn together separately, with the seam allowances away from the wearer; the silk back is lapped by the side pieces (which are themselves pieced), topstitched with green silk thread through all the layers, and the fronts lap the sides. The front lining is free from the silk except at the side seams and armholes, darted once on either side and hemmed towards the wearer. The silk is hemmed at the neckline with room for a drawstring, and hemmed normally at the bottom; 2.5cm (1in) above the bottom the silk is slightly tucked to the outside to hold another drawstring. The lining strap is turned out and whipped to the hemmed front, while the silk strap is roughly 2cm (¾in) longer and topstitched over the silk front. At the back of the neck there is a narrow facing of brown polished cotton (cotton sateen). The sleeve, lined in brown polished cotton (cotton sateen), has a 4cm (1½in) hem at the wrist.

The skirt is cut in six pieces: two slightly flared ones for the apron, two narrow side panels, and two rectangles for the back. The side panels and front pieces are seamed only up to the mark. The front pieces are sewn to the folded band, through which runs a tape drawstring. The side panels and back pieces are backstitched to the back and side pieces 6cm (2½in) from the bottom edge of the bodice.

*Left: **Quaker gown courtesy of the New York State Historical Association, Cooperstown, NY (N91-52). This detail shows the inside of the back.***

Right: *The Religious Society of Friends (Quakers) deliberately avoided the vanities of the world, including ladies fashions, so their clothing style fell behind. No high waistlines for them, then, just a neat and rather old-fashioned style. This portrait is of Elizabeth Fry, prison reformer, quaker and philanthropist.*

Regency Women's Dress

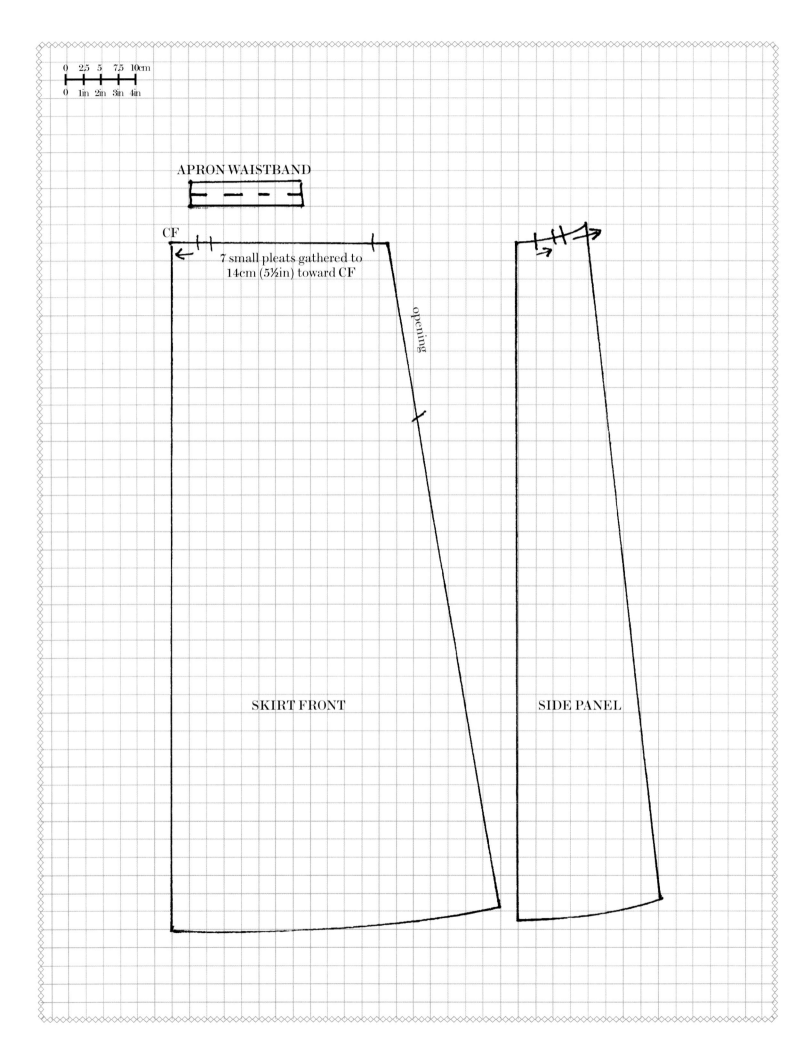

0  2.5  5  7.5  10cm
0  1in 2in 3in 4in

APRON WAISTBAND

CF

7 small pleats gathered to
14cm (5½in) toward CF

opening

SKIRT FRONT

SIDE PANEL

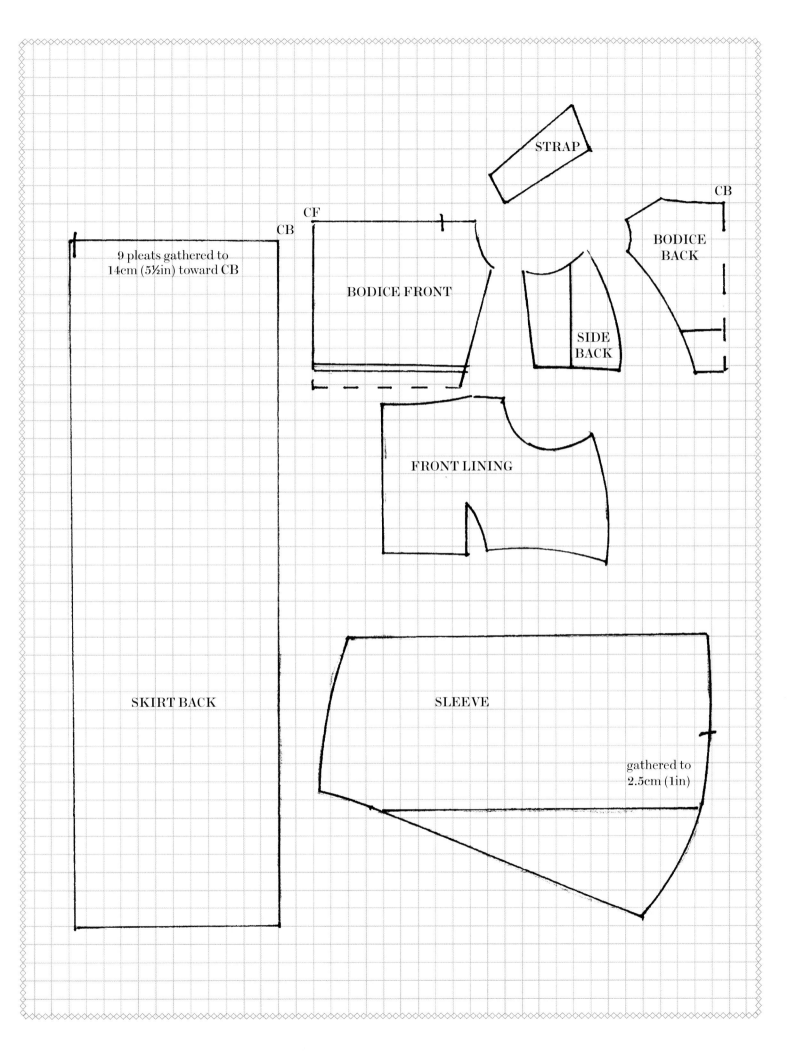

STRAP

CF

CB

BODICE FRONT

CB

BODICE BACK

SIDE BACK

9 pleats gathered to 14cm (5½in) toward CB

CB

FRONT LINING

SKIRT BACK

SLEEVE

gathered to 2.5cm (1in)

# Morning Dress
## 1813–1816

This cotton morning dress was worn by Isabella Lenox (1789–1866), who married William Banks (1782–1848) in 1823.

The fabric of the unlined gown is cotton, printed densely with yellow stars and purplish-grey clouds. The front bodice piece is darted, with the darts turned toward the centre and topstitched; the front is lapped over the sides and topstitched, and the sides over the backs. The neckline is piped and bound with a cotton print bias binding. The short oversleeve is bound and piped like the neckline. This oversleeve is trimmed with 4cm (1½in) wide ruffles whip-gathered to the fabric along the dotted lines. The long undersleeve is trimmed with two ruffles on the broken lines and

another at the wrist. Both sleeves are sewn together into a piped armhole.

The front panel of the skirt is lapped and topstitched to the bodice, and the back panels are backstitched; the whole skirt attachment is backed with a tape. The lower edge is finished with a 5cm (2in) hem.

4.5cm (1¾in) wide ruffles trim the bottom of the skirt along the broken and plain lines: the plain lines indicate ruffles headed with piping. The centre-back seam is open down to the mark, where it is heavily overcast with white thread on either side of and across the juncture. The gown fastens with hooks and eyes on the neckline and at the top of the skirt.

Left: *Cotton morning dress courtesy of the Albany Institute of History and Art, Albany, NY (1972.95.5).*

Right: *Fashion plate for Costume Parisien (1816) of a woman wearing nineteenth century morning dress. Like our dress, this pale blue robe is ornamented on the bodice, cuffs and hem with narrow pinked flounces (volans).*

Regency Women's Dress

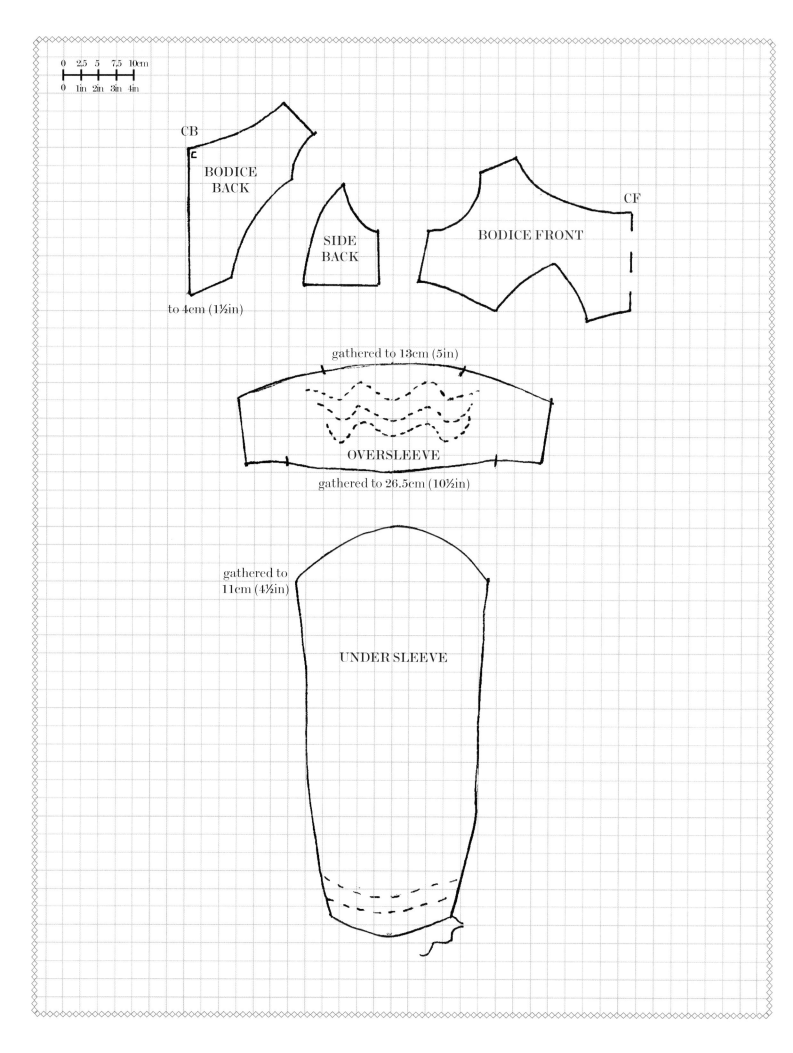

0 2.5 5 7.5 10cm
0 1in 2in 3in 4in

CB

BODICE
BACK

to 4cm (1½in)

SIDE
BACK

BODICE FRONT

CF

gathered to 13cm (5in)

OVERSLEEVE

gathered to 26.5cm (10½in)

gathered to
11cm (4½in)

UNDER SLEEVE

0 2.5 5 7.5 10cm
0 1in 2in 3in 4in

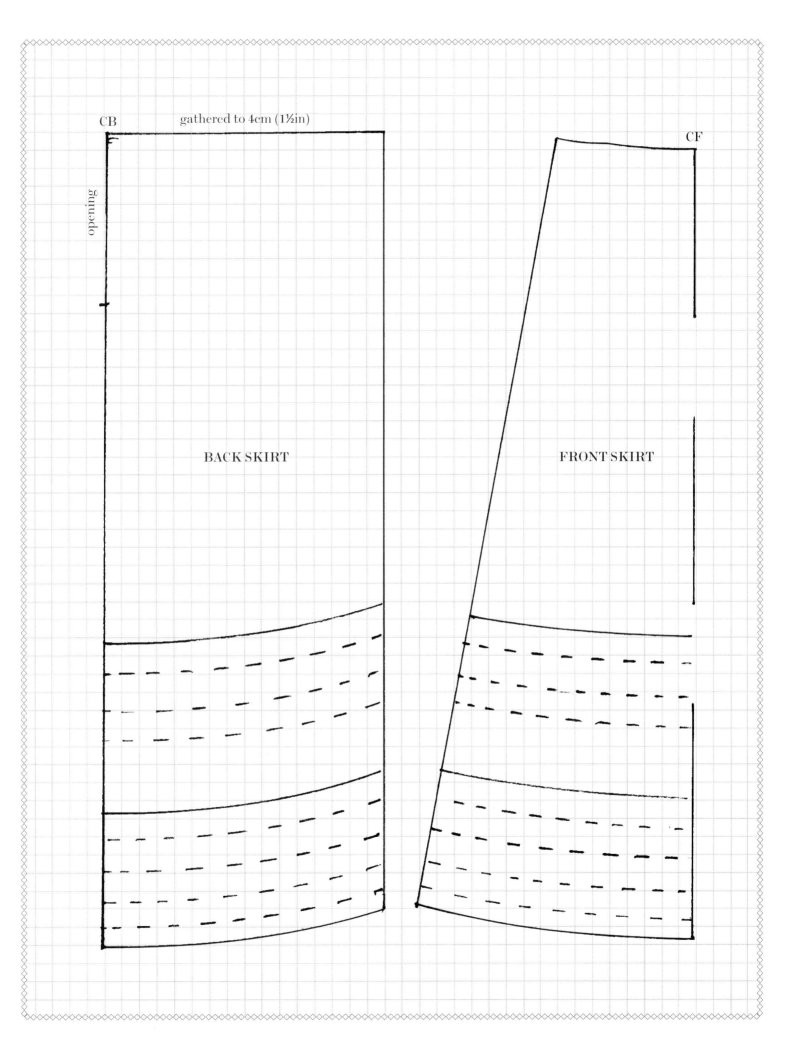

CB

gathered to 4cm (1½in)

CF

opening

BACK SKIRT

FRONT SKIRT

# Evening Dress
## 1812–1817

This dress is provenanced to Mary Crosby Jordan (1794–1864), of Walkill, New York. It is of an almost-opaque white cotton, lined and embroidered with white linen.

Like many of the other dresses, this one is fully lined in the side bodice pieces and partially lined in the back pieces, from the side seam to the broken line. The front piece is embroidered as shown, with Xs outlined in French knots, curving lines in sets of three, also in French knots, and five-petalled flowers in satin stitch, with centres in French knots. The top edge is hemmed to admit a 2mm (¹/sin) tape as a drawstring, which emerges from an eyelet at the centre front inside the hem to tie in a bow. The front-side and back-side seams are backstitched, the seam allowances overcast; the strap is cut with the selvedge on the neckline and is sandwiched between the cotton and linen on both ends and topstitched. The back neckline is also hemmed to admit a 1cm (³/sin) drawstring; no method of fastening remains at the waist. The bottom of the sleeve is bound with a 28cm (11in) long band, 1cm (³/sin) wide when folded: the exterior edge is backstitched to the sleeve, and the interior is whipped.

The front panel of the skirt and the side panel are sewn flat to the bodice (the front marked where the edge of the front bodice panel attaches to it). The back opening runs down to the mark, where a small piece of white tape binds the join in the fabric. The entire skirt is backstitched to the bodice. The tucks in the skirt are a little more irregular than they are drawn, but overall the upper tuck covers the lower one, and is sewn with larger running stitches. Below the tucks the skirt is heavily embroidered in satin stitches, with French knots indicated by small dots. The larger dots forming loops and swags beneath the plant and flower motifs indicate much larger knot stitches, or bubbles. The hem is 4.5cm (1¾in) deep, ending just at the bottom of the knotted swags.

Left: *White cotton dress courtesy of the New York State Museum, Albany, NY (2004.65.2). This detail of the bodice shows the French knot and satin stitch embroidery on the front.*

Right: *'The Living Corbeille'*,
Le Bon Genre *(1817)*
*showing white cotton robes*
*with short puffed sleeves*
*and embroidered hems.*

Regency Women's Dress

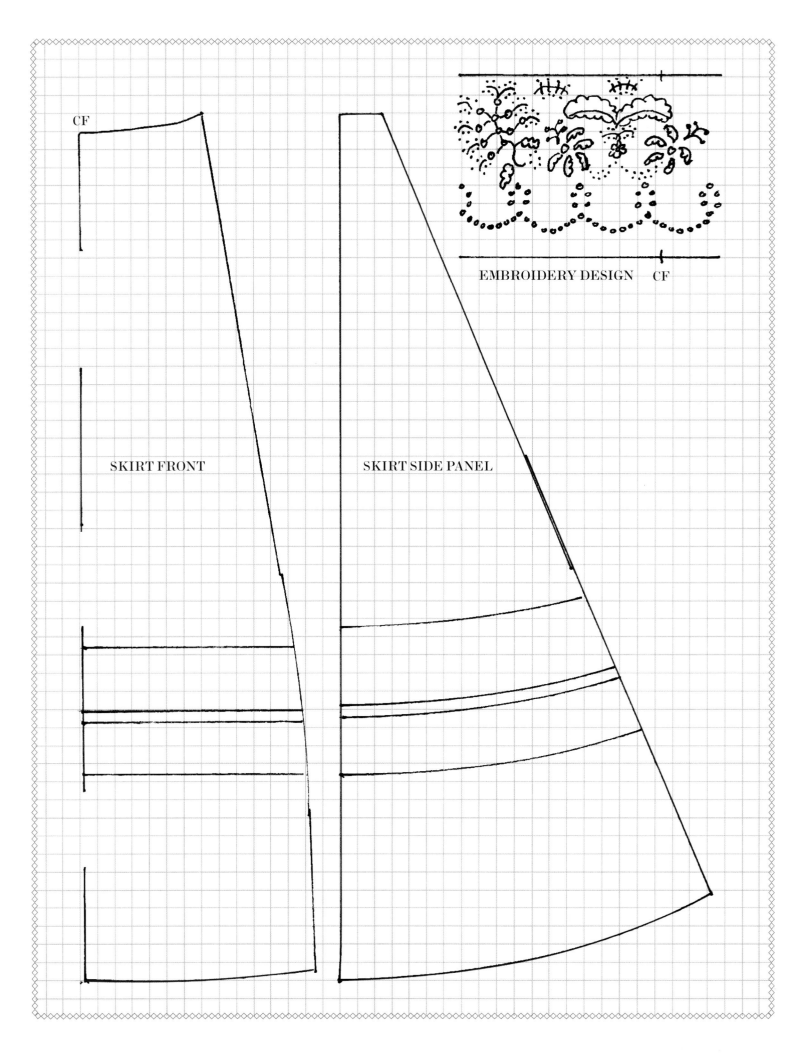

CF

SKIRT FRONT

SKIRT SIDE PANEL

EMBROIDERY DESIGN     CF

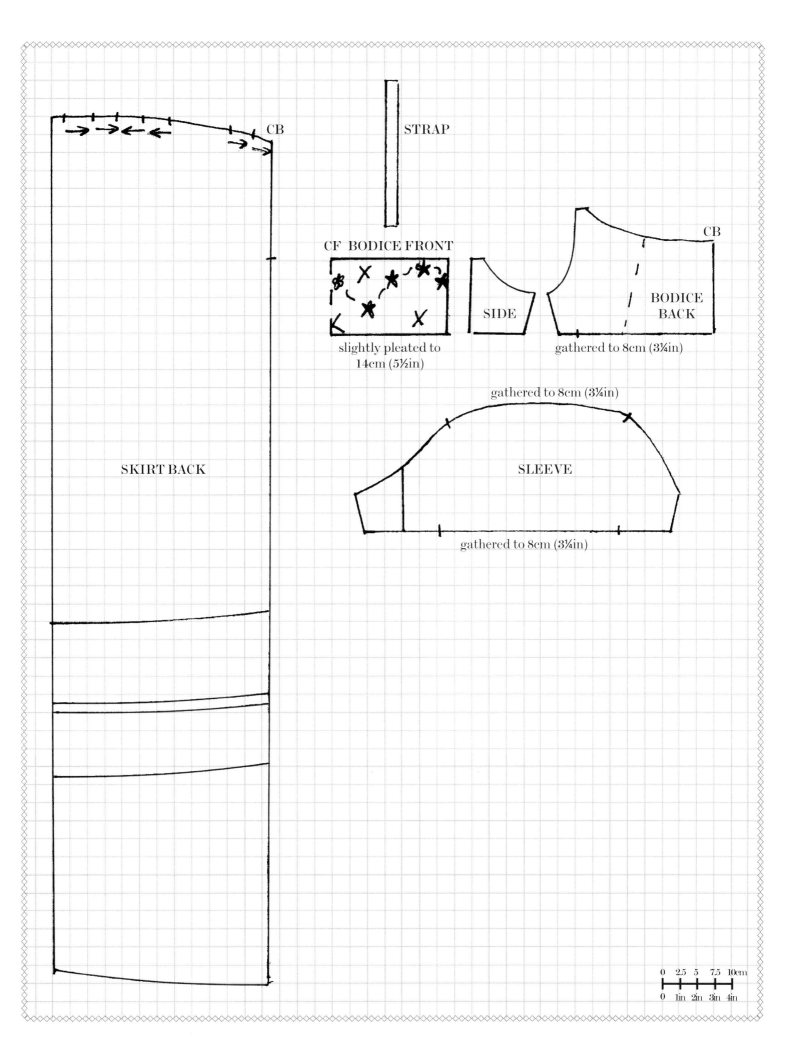

CB

STRAP

CF BODICE FRONT

CB

SIDE

BODICE BACK

slightly pleated to 14cm (5½in)

gathered to 8cm (3¼in)

gathered to 8cm (3¼in)

SKIRT BACK

SLEEVE

gathered to 8cm (3¼in)

0   2.5   5   7.5   10cm

0   1in  2in  3in  4in

# Evening Dress

## 1819–1821

This dress was worn by Ann Eliza Ten Eyck (1806–1866) around the time of her marriage to James Ten Eyck in 1821. The silk of the dress is figured with sprigs, and is striped with dark and light gold, shading into each other. The piping and appliqués are a dull gold or tan satin with a light hand.

The bodice is lined with a fine linen. The front and side pieces are one in the lining; the front is lapped over the sides and topstitched through the linen. The linen and silk are darted together, the darts pressed toward the centre and topstitched, while the other edges are whipped to the lining. The back pieces are flatlined, and seamed to the sides with piping, and the shoulder seams are also piped. Three-leafed satin motifs are placed along the darts and on the armhole: Xs mark their bases, and Os the tips of the leaves that are tacked down. The leaves on the bodice are 6cm (2½in) long (indicated by straight lines) and 9cm (3½in) long (indicated by wavy lines); all the leaves are bound with satin bias binding and gathered very tightly at their bases. The back originally had a hook and eye at the top with ties running through the channels at the bottom.

The sleeves are highly complicated puffs, with each seam piped. On the underside of the arm is a relatively square piece that is attached to the armhole at one end and to the sleeve band at the other; there are two equilateral triangles of figured silk sewn into the armhole and a strip of three triangles sewn into the band, placed so that the triangles on the upper edge match the recesses in the strip. The long satin binding runs between the upper and lower triangles, the short ends attached to the sides of the square. It is gathered as necessary at each corner on each side. Two brown silk gimp knots are attached at the point of each triangle, resting on the satin. The lower edge is piped in satin and bound with a strip of figured silk. The rear edge of the square lines up with the piped side-back seam of the bodice.

The skirt is sewn together with running stitches, the narrow, scalloped tabs sewn into the seam from A to B. The tabs are edged with piping, as is the A-to-B seam, and gimp knots are placed on each scallop, so that they angle with the grain and point slightly down; only the first scallop lacks a knot. Each side of the back is whipped to the bodice, which is turned up to form the aforementioned channel. The rest of the skirt is topstitched to the bodice. The hem is 6cm (2½in) high. Sinuous broken lines indicate bias bands of satin, seamed into tubes and folded so that the seam is visible. The bands are decorated with more leaf appliqués, these 9cm (3½in) and 11.5cm (4½in) long (the latter indicated with broken lines); their gathered raw edges are hidden under the band. The six-leafed motifs are trimmed with a gimp knot in the centre, over the band.

Left: *Gold formal dress
courtesy of the Albany
Institute of History and Art,
Albany, NY (1938.3.1). The
puff sleeves are complicated
and highly decorated.*

Right: *Evening dress featured
in Ackermann's Repository
(1823). A charming pink and
white dress with two deep rows
of decoration at the hem. The
sleeves are short and full with a
vandyked design.*

Regency Women's Dress

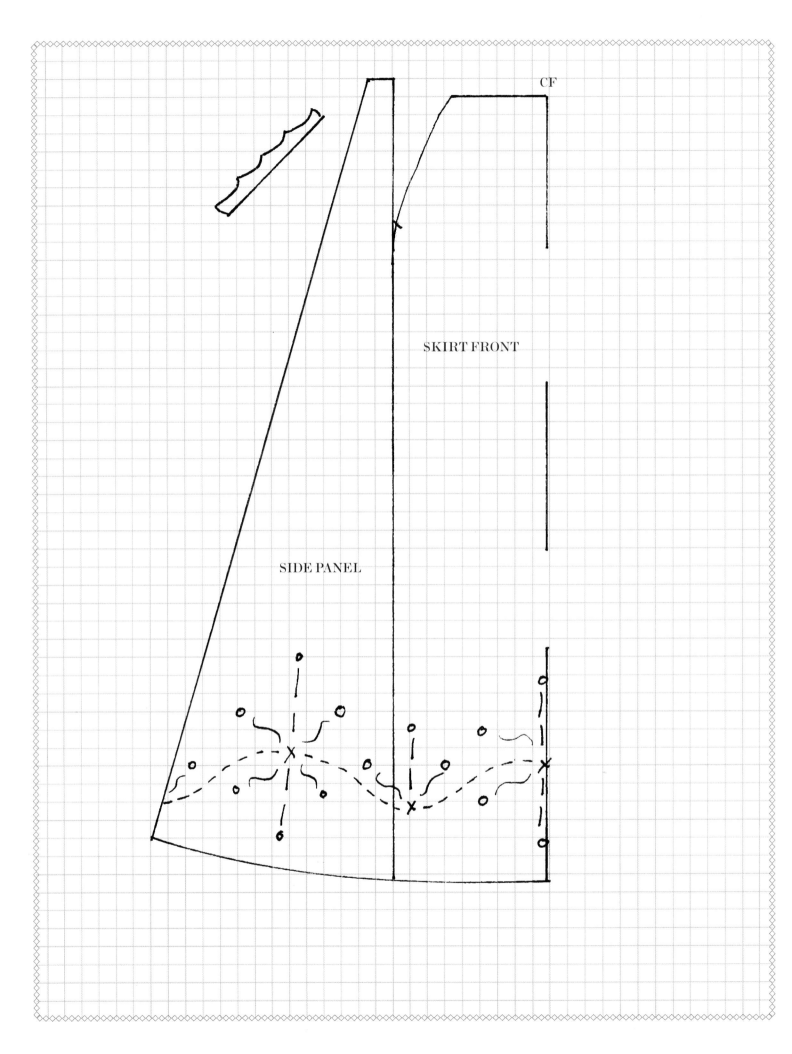

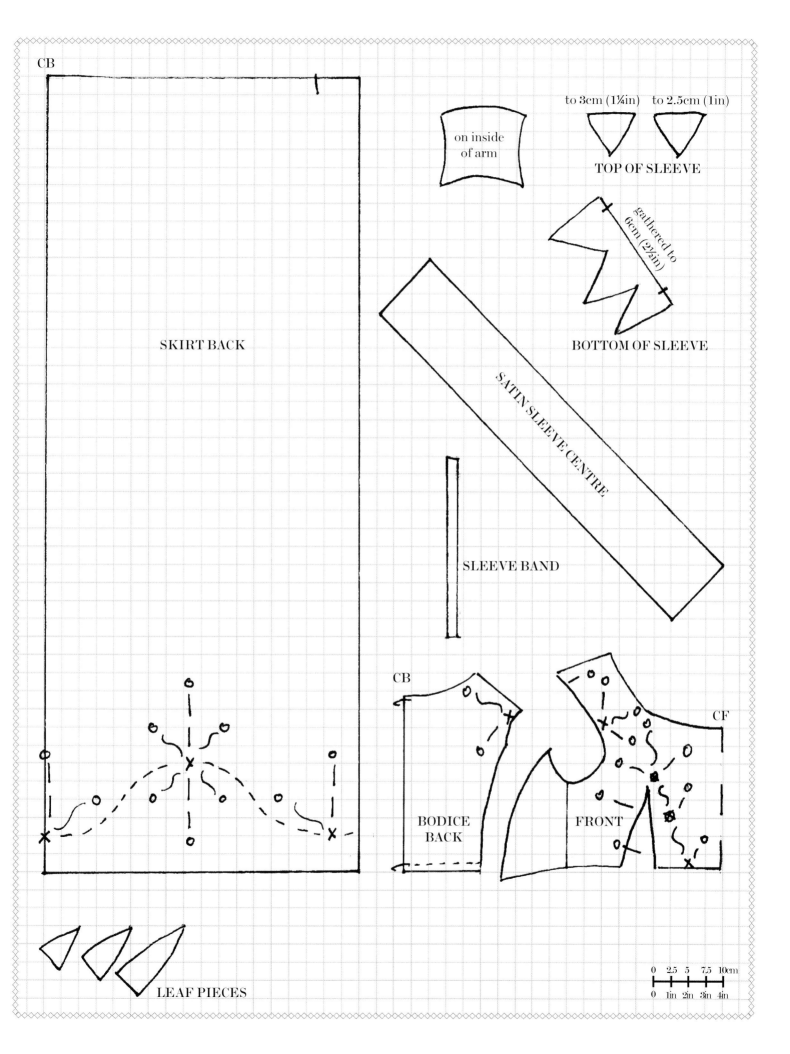

CB

SKIRT BACK

on inside
of arm

to 3cm (1¼in)    to 2.5cm (1in)

TOP OF SLEEVE

gathered to
6cm (2½in)

BOTTOM OF SLEEVE

SATIN SLEEVE CENTRE

SLEEVE BAND

CB

CF

BODICE
BACK

FRONT

0   2.5   5   7.5   10cm

0   1in   2in   3in   4in

LEAF PIECES

# Evening Dress
## 1818–1820

While other short-sleeved gowns could have been worn during the day or evening, the silver embellishments on the cotton mean that this would have been appropriate for very formal occasions. Its sheerness makes it a likely ball dress, worn over a white or coloured silk 'slip'. It is said to have been included in the trousseau of Elizabeth Mary Douglas (1799–1852) on her 1822 marriage to James Monroe, Jr. (1799–1870). While she may have taken it with her, it was almost certainly not intended for her to wear to a formal occasion, as it would have been rather out of date.

The whole gown is made of a sheer cotton mull, stamped with silver lamella in diagonal lines; the lamella are twisted around to hold the fabric. There is only a small strip of a heavier cotton lining sewn around the armhole, and in the side piece; a length of tape runs around the outer edge of the armhole lining. The mull side piece is lapped over the front and back and topstitched in place, as is the shoulder piece. The front is darted, with the darts turned towards the centre, and topstitched. The entire neckline is hemmed with room for a narrow tape drawstring to fasten it at the top. The back waist fastens with a hook and eye, and both sides of the centre-back edges are backed with a white tape. The sleeve head is backstitched into the armhole with large stitches, the seam allowances overcast. The lower edge of the sleeve is hemmed, with an eyelet placed where marked to allow the drawstring that would puff the sleeve to be tied.

The skirt is lapped over and topstitched to the bodice from the centre front to the marks on the back panels; the back panels are backstitched to the bodice. A white tape backs the entire skirt-bodice seam. The side skirt panel and back piece are tucked where marked, before the front panel is attached to them.

The bottom of the skirt was embroidered with *boteh* or paisley motifs in silver threads and silver lamella after the dress was made up. Below the *botehs* is a row of lamella dots between two thin lines of silver thread, and below this register the dress is cut in small zigzags, each zigzag embellished with six lamella dots and edged with silver thread 'vines'. The lower edge is faced with the white lining cotton to just below the *botehs*.

Left: *Cotton formal dress courtesy of the New York State Historical Association, Cooperstown, NY (N217-1962). The hem is embroidered with* boteh, *or paisley, motifs.*

Right: *A fashionable couple perform the first quadrille at Almack's, London (c.1815). Even formal Regency dresses have a relaxed, comfortable styling. Compared with the style before and after the period, the dresses were loose and unrestricting.*

Regency Women's Dress

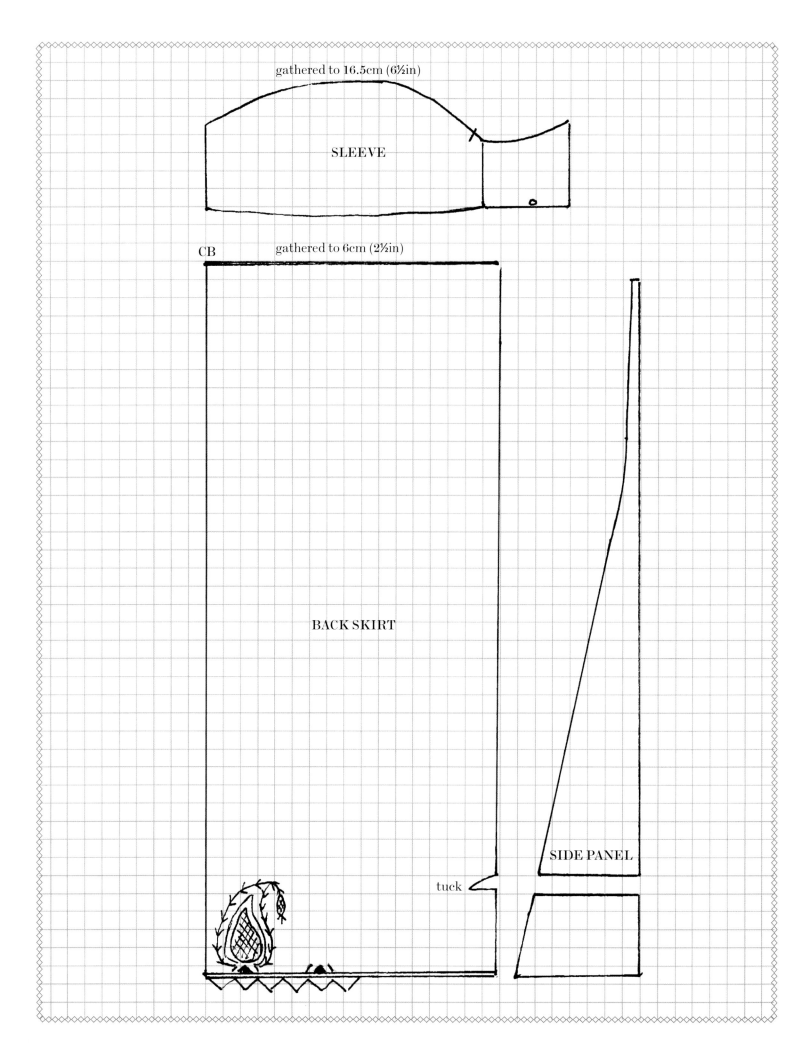

gathered to 16.5cm (6½in)

SLEEVE

CB    gathered to 6cm (2½in)

BACK SKIRT

SIDE PANEL

tuck

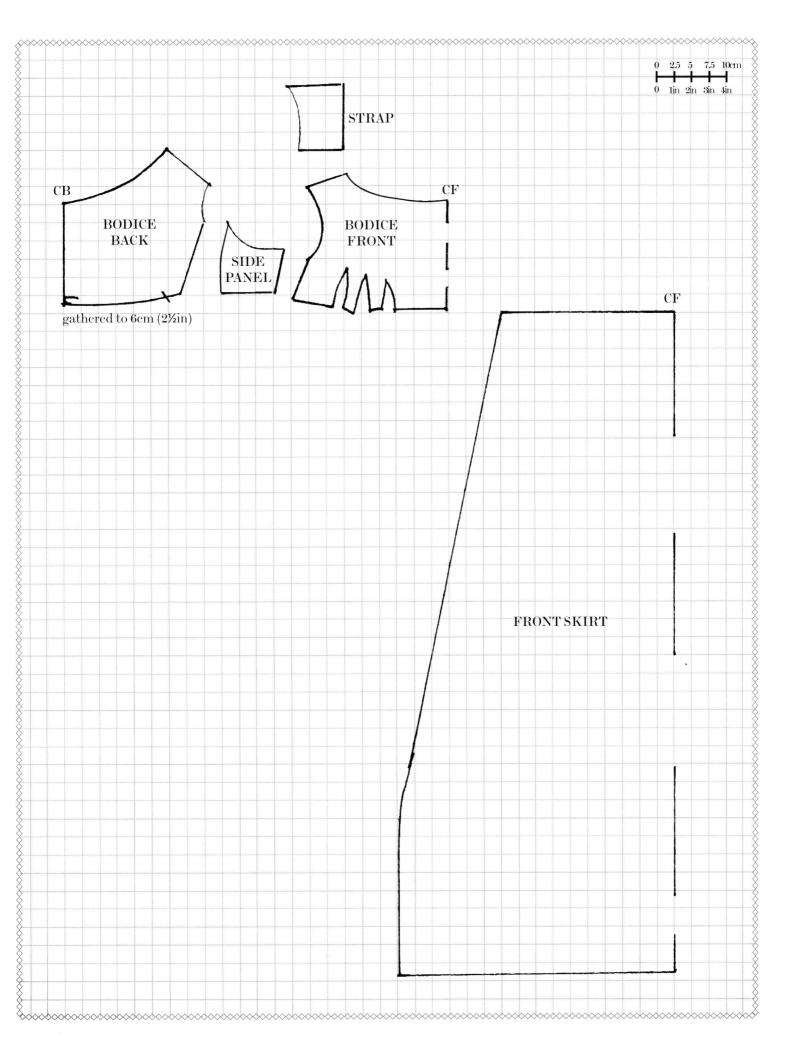

STRAP

CB

BODICE
BACK

CF

SIDE
PANEL

BODICE
FRONT

gathered to 6cm (2½in)

CF

FRONT SKIRT

CF

0  2.5  5  7.5  10cm

0  1in  2in  3in  4in

0  2.5  5  7.5  10cm

0  1in  2in  3in  4in

# Formal Dress
## 1818–1822

The family tradition relating to this dotted Swiss gown is that it was made for Anna Pratt Rice (1785–1876), and might have been worn for her wedding in 1806; however, the level of the waist and the shape of the sleeves are too late for that date. A niece, Mary Ann Pratt Brother (1808–1883), is said to have possibly worn it to her wedding in 1826, but by that date the sleeves would have seemed ludicrously small and the waist too high. It is most likely that it was worn by Anna Pratt Rice ten or more years after her wedding, or else by a different ancestor of the donor.

The bodice is unlined except for the side piece, which is flatlined with a heavier white cotton, and the back, where the lining is free at the neckline and only extends to the broken vertical line. The deep darts in the front are turned to the centre and topstitched. The front piece is lapped and topstitched over the side piece, while the side-back seam is piped and backstitched, as is the shoulder seam. At the bottom of the back is a drawstring to fasten the gown, but no method of closure remains at the top. The neckline is edged with piping (as is the armhole) and then bound. The slashes and puffs in the sleeves are piped as well, the puffs gathered all around to fit into the slashes.

The front skirt panel is topstitched to the bodice up to the mark, and then backstitched, and the skirt is open down the back to the mark. The hem is faced with a 16.5cm (6½in) band of white cotton.

Left: *Detail of sleeve from a white dotted Swiss dress courtesy of the New York State Historical Association, Cooperstown, NY (N800-1963).*

Right: *Hand-coloured fashion plate for* Young Lady's Pocket Magazine, *December 1824. Notice how far the waist has dropped, although the puffed sleeves of the Empire style remain in fashion for formal or evening wear at least.*

Regency Women's Dress

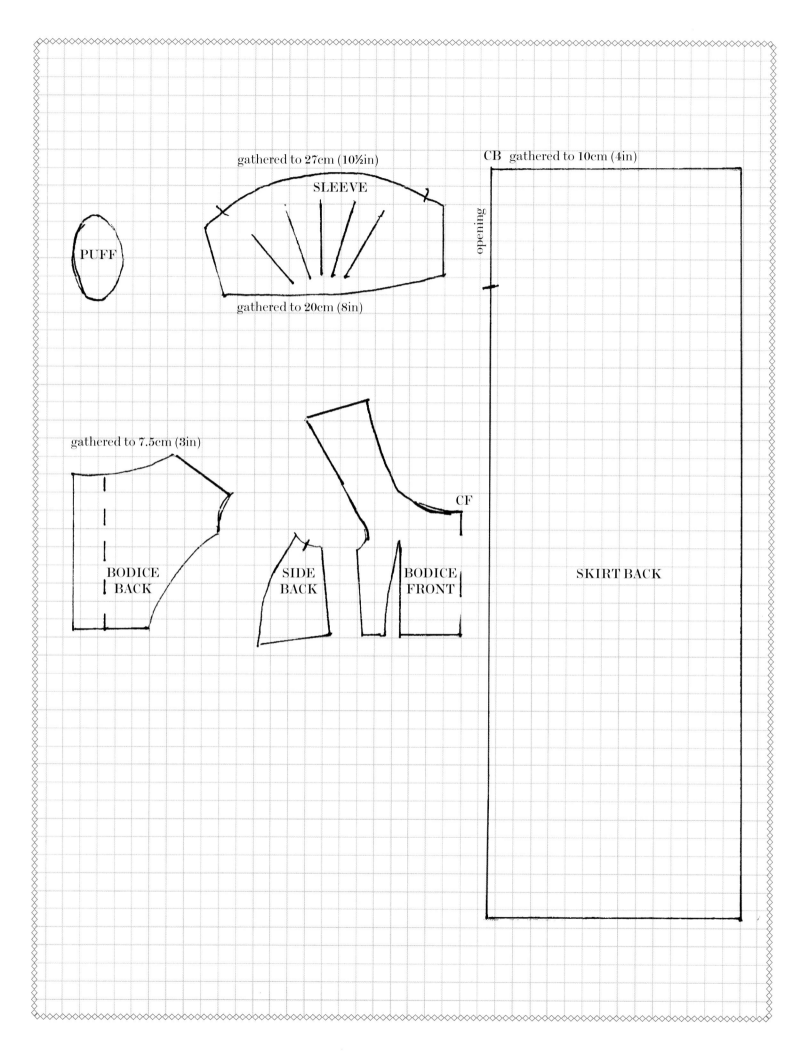

gathered to 27cm (10½in)

SLEEVE

CB  gathered to 10cm (4in)

opening

gathered to 20cm (8in)

PUFF

gathered to 7.5cm (3in)

BODICE
BACK

SIDE
BACK

BODICE
FRONT

CF

SKIRT BACK

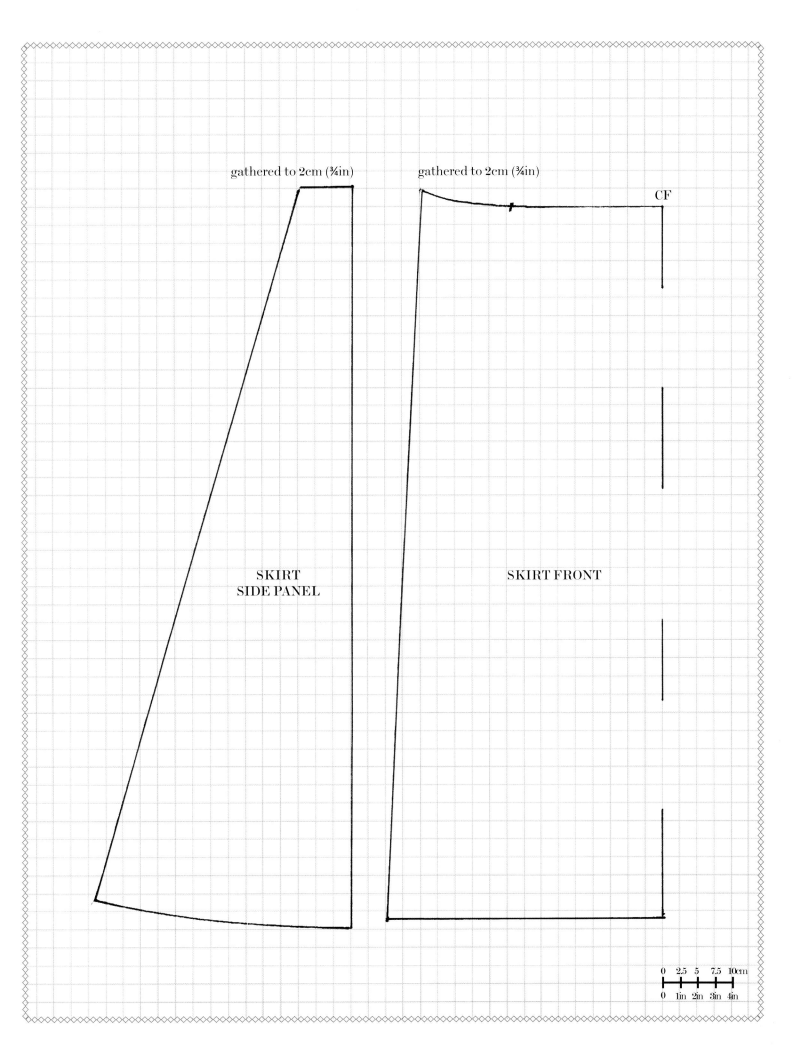

gathered to 2cm (¾in)

gathered to 2cm (¾in)

CF

SKIRT
SIDE PANEL

SKIRT FRONT

0   2.5   5   7.5   10cm

0   1in   2in   3in   4in

# Bodice of an Evening Dress
## 1819–1823

The front piece of the bodice is unlined; the dart pairs are turned away from each other and topstitched with backstitches. The front piece laps the curved shoulder strap, which is also unlined, and is topstitched in place. The stomacher is cut of dark pink gauze, striped on the lines with white satin bias bands; the side edges are bound, and then the top edge, and the corners are trimmed with buttons covered intricately with white and pink silk. The whole is tacked down, the bottom edge turned back up to the interior of the bodice. The back and side pieces are lined with a polished white linen, the side piece of the lining extending 4cm (1½in) into the front piece. The side-back seam is backstitched in the lining, with the seam allowances turned away from the wearer; in the silk, the side piece is lapped over the back and topstitched. This seam is covered

with a white silk cord, which appears twisted as it has been tightly whipped with matching thread. The strap and back silk and lining are seamed with the seam allowances toward the wearer, and the seam is covered with the same cord. The back silk and lining pieces are separate from each other apart from the seam; a white tape is whipped inside the bottom edge of the front piece, the sides and the back lining, the bottom of the stomacher turning up over the tape. The lining fastens at centre back with three hooks and eyes. On the exterior, the bottom of the bodice is covered with a waistband of pink silk satin, folded double down the length and bound on all edges with bias bands of white satin, which is attached with large basting stitches; the back pleats are held by this waistband. The bodice fastens at the neckline with a drawstring, and at the waist with a hook and eye on the waistband. The back lining piece is finished at the neckline with a hem, while the rest of the neckline is bound with white satin; above the stomacher, the binding is not finished on the inside, but hangs down to the width of 2.5cm (1in) with a raw edge.

The sleeves are made on a foundation of pink satin, pleated slightly at the lower edge as shown. The layer over it, of dark pink gauze, is irregularly pleated and gathered to fit the upper and lower edges of the foundation sleeve. The gauze is covered by two triangular gauze petals, edged with a 2.5cm (1in) wide white gauze bias band, and trimmed on the broken line and the edge of the pink gauze with white satin, the corners trimmed on the white gauze with the same buttons as the stomacher, placed on the O marks. The upper edge of the petals overlap over the top of the arm to the mark. The bottom of the two sleeve layers is finished with a pink satin cuff, piped in white satin, and lined with layers of pink and white gauze.

Left: *Bodice with stomacher courtesy of the Albany Institute of History and Art, Albany, NY (U1980.22). This detail shows the interior of the back.*

Right: *Around this time dresses were becoming more and more ornate, especially at the neckline and sleeves and sometimes also at the hem, as shown in this hand-coloured fashion plate for* Young Lady's Pocket Magazine *(1824). This pale yellow gown has short, puffed sleeves and a hem decorated with two rouleaux infilled with 'puffings' and oval-shaped designs, topped with paisley pattern trim.*

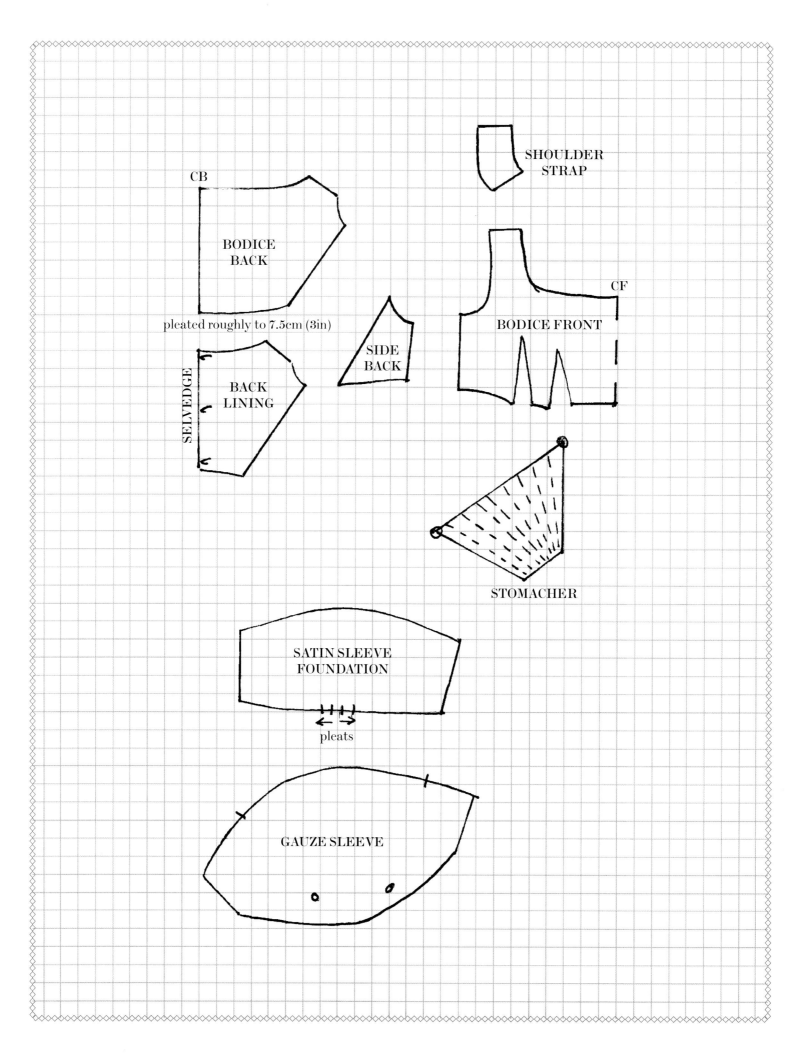

CB

SHOULDER
STRAP

BODICE
BACK

CF

pleated roughly to 7.5cm (3in)

SELVEDGE

BACK
LINING

SIDE
BACK

BODICE FRONT

STOMACHER

SATIN SLEEVE
FOUNDATION

pleats

GAUZE SLEEVE

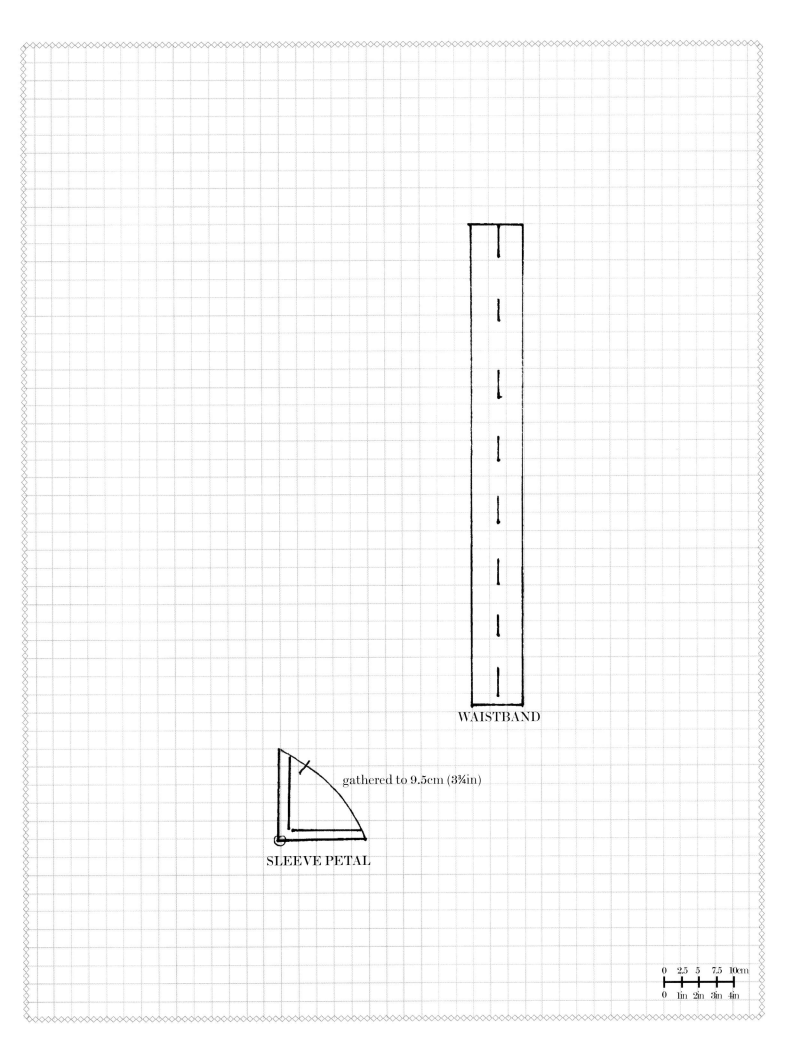

WAISTBAND

gathered to 9.5cm (3¾in)

SLEEVE PETAL

# Ball Dress
## 1820–1825

Like many gowns intended for dancing at evening entertainments during this era, this gown is unlined and somewhat sheer, made from an ivory silk crepe, and would have been worn over a slip. It is believed to have been worn at a ball celebrating the opening of the Erie Canal in 1821.

The bodice of the gown is made of two layers of crepe treated as one, with a soft cotton lining added at some later point. The side back pieces were lapped over the back pieces and backstitched; the front pieces were then lapped and backstitched over the side pieces. There is a narrow tape running through the back neckline, tying to fasten the gown, and a plain linen tape facing the whole neckline. The whole bodice is sewn with a running stitch to a single-layer linen waistband, the seam allowances along the top and bottom of which are unfinished and pressed open. There are two hooks on the right end of the waistband, meeting eyes (no longer present) on the other end. The sleeves are one layer, the crepe cuff folded in half to bind the lower edge. The skirt is made of five identical rectangles, gathered to the linen waistband evenly except at the centre front, where the gathering is slightly lighter. There is a tuck near the 5cm (2in) hem, indicated by solid lines.

The gown is adorned with satin decorations: bias-cut pink satin strips cut in zigzags and piped on the edges, called *dents de loup* in French fashion publications, and pink and white satin 'chains'. The *dents de loup* are indicated by dashed lines on the bodice and skirt; they are lightly padded on the skirt. The chains are made from a 12mm (½in) white cotton cord covered by the satin, with the larger loops in pink satin and the smaller loops linking the pink ones in white. These are arranged on the dotted lines beneath the *dents de loup* on the skirt, along the bottom of the *dents* on the bodice, around the neckline, down the right side of the back bodice opening, and around the sleeve cuffs. (The chains on the skirt are backed with a white net, most likely to help hold out the skirt, like the padded *dents*.)

There is a separate pink satin belt that would cover the plain linen waistband. With a deep point at the centre front, it probably would have been called a '*belt à la Marie Stuart*' or after another historical reference, as the style was drawn from portraits of past centuries. The belt is cut on the bias, piped on the edges, and backed with linen cut on the straight of grain, interlined with a stiffer material. The slightly angled end holds metal eyes; the hooks are on the underside of the belt, at the marks near the pointed end.

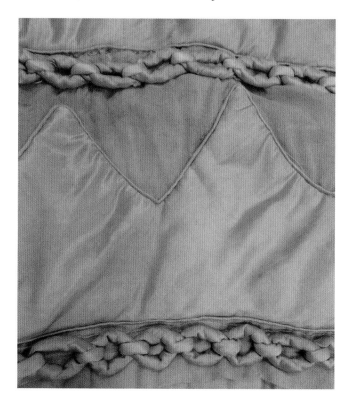

*Left: Crepe ball dress courtesy of the Historic Cherry Hill Collection, Albany, NY (3717a-b). The gown is adorned with satin decorations, as seen on this detail of the hem.*

*Right: Hand-coloured fashion plate for* Young Lady's Pocket Magazine, *October 1824. The lower waistline and elaborate decorations on the neck, sleeves and hem signal the end of the Regency period. Although still elegant, the styling is much more ornate.*

Regency Women's Dress

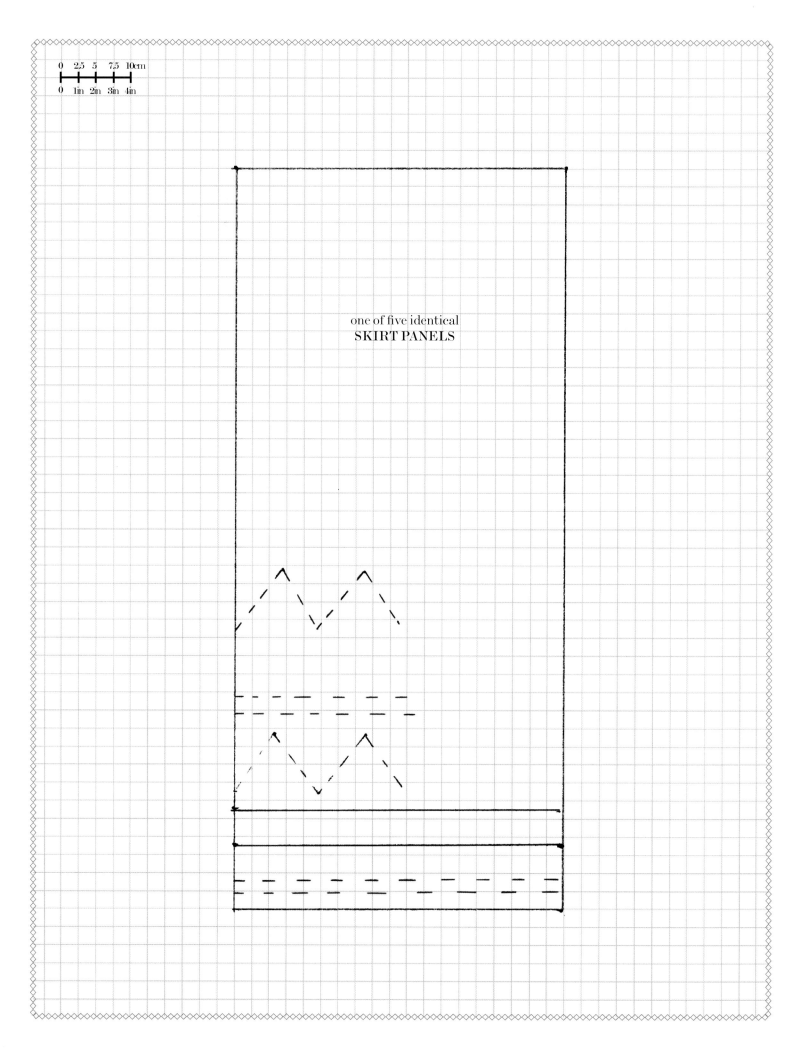

one of five identical
**SKIRT PANELS**

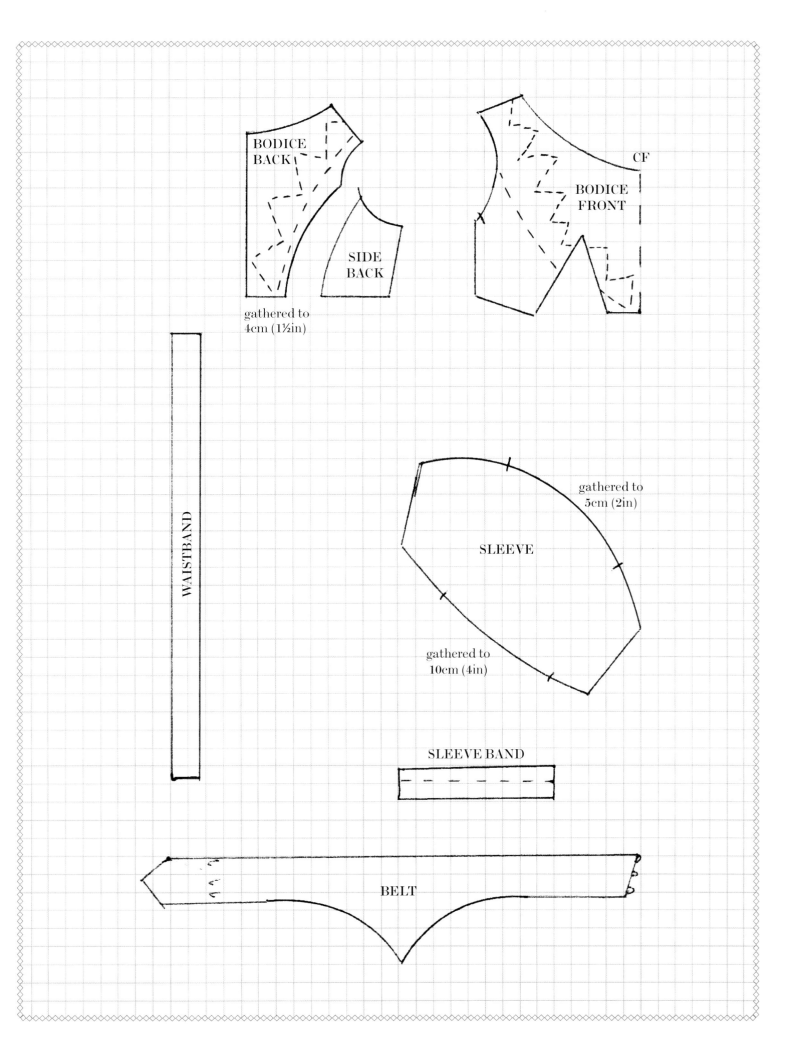

BODICE
BACK

SIDE
BACK

CF

BODICE
FRONT

gathered to
4cm (1½in)

WAISTBAND

gathered to
5cm (2in)

SLEEVE

gathered to
10cm (4in)

SLEEVE BAND

BELT

# Morning Dress
## 1823–1826

The bodice of this sheer green checked silk dress is unlined except under and around the armhole, and the waist- and neckbands, where it is lined in linen. The front is lapped over the back pieces and topstitched in green silk through the lining. The bodice is sandwiched between the waistband and its lining and topstitched. The neckline is finished with straight bands of checked silk, 12mm (½in) wide, piped with green silk taffeta: the front band is 35.5cm (14in) and the back ones are each 16.5cm (6½in) each, overlapping at the ends over the armholes, to which they form the upper edge. The neckline is trimmed with triangles of checked silk, bound with green taffeta: six across the front of the neckline, three on either side of the back, and two gathered slightly over the sleeve.

The sleeve is set into a piped armhole so that its seam is just slightly behind the bodice side seam.

The bottom of the sleeve is open to the marks and is trimmed with a self-fabric cuff, which has a hook and eye near the seam to fasten it. The cuff is trimmed with a decoration cut from the checked silk and bound with taffeta, inserted into the seam between the cuff and sleeve.

The top of the skirt is pleated as shown on the pattern then folded inside. The edge is overcast, and the whole whipped to the bottom of the waistband. The lower edge is finished with a thick piping, and above the piping the skirt is tucked as marked. The bottom of the skirt is also trimmed with a flat ruffle of bias-cut checked silk, piped along the top and the bottom. The top is cut in scallops as marked on the pattern; the lower edge is cut in tabs, also as marked, and the corners of these tabs are folded up and to the centre of each to form points.

Left: *Silk dress courtesy of Old Sturbridge Village, Sturbridge, MA (26.33.63). This detail shows the trimmed cuff.*

Right: *A pink and white striped gown with long, full sleeves and four flounces at the hem. Hand-coloured engraving for the Lady's Magazine (1826).*

Regency Women's Dress

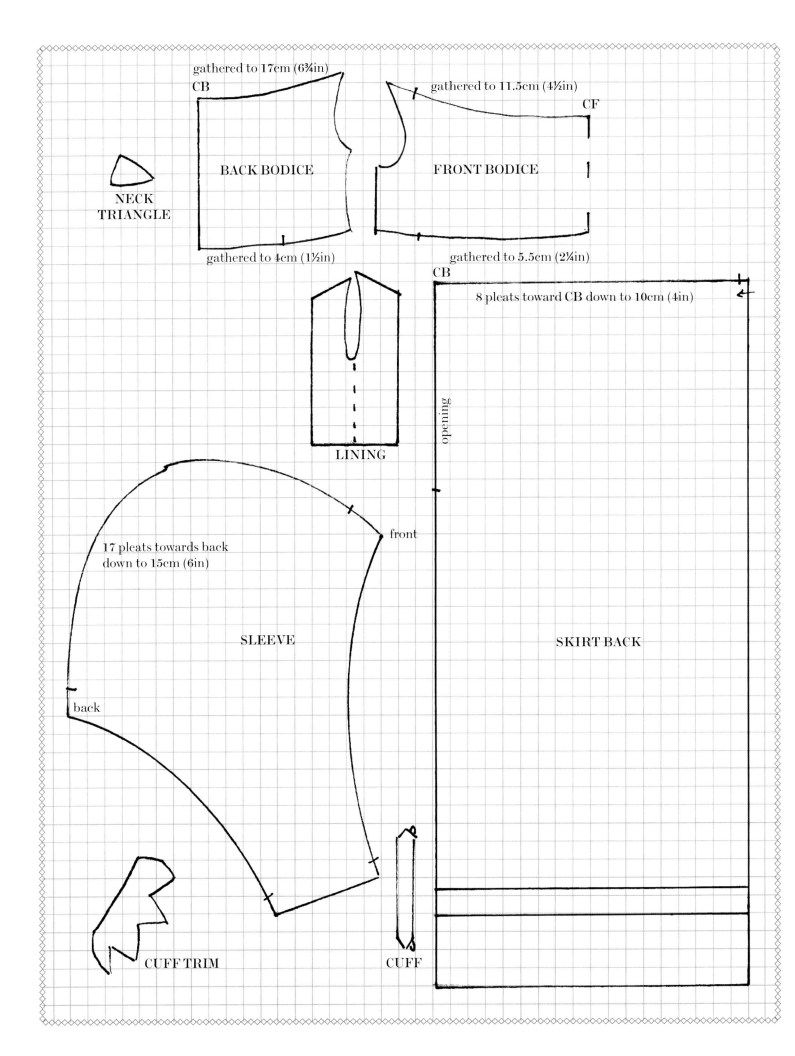

gathered to 17cm (6¾in)

CB

gathered to 11.5cm (4½in)

CF

BACK BODICE

FRONT BODICE

NECK TRIANGLE

gathered to 4cm (1½in)

gathered to 5.5cm (2¼in)

CB

8 pleats toward CB down to 10cm (4in)

opening

LINING

17 pleats towards back down to 15cm (6in)

front

SLEEVE

SKIRT BACK

back

CUFF TRIM

CUFF

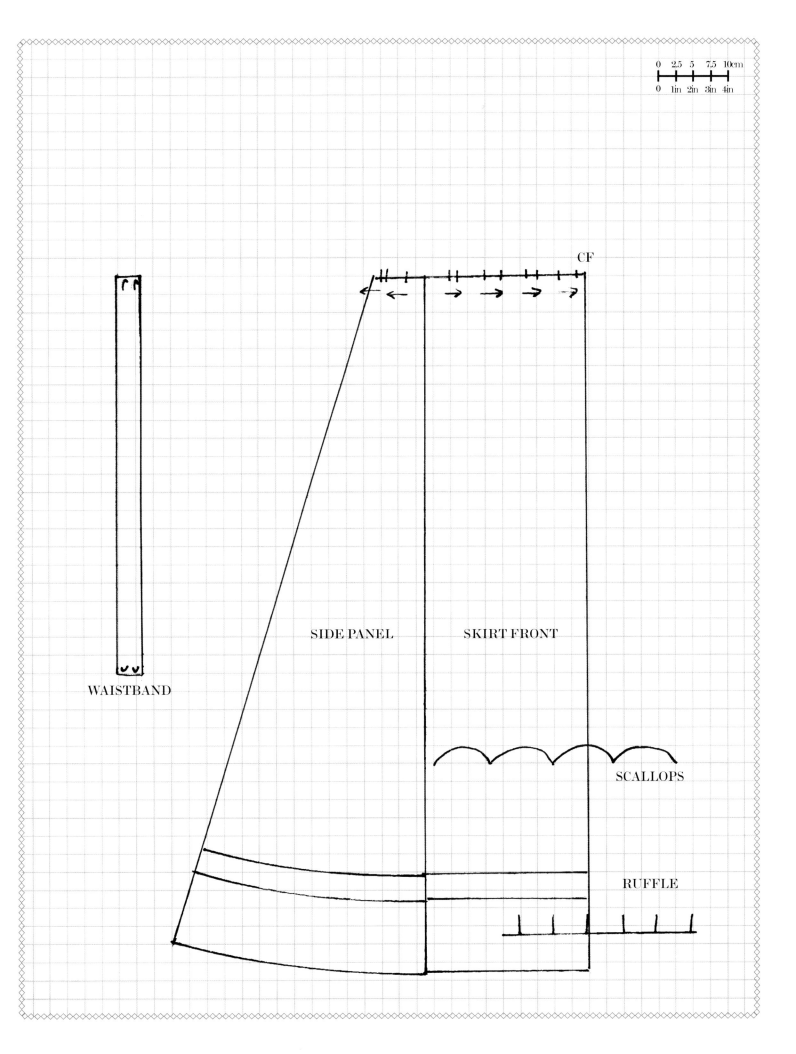

WAISTBAND

SIDE PANEL

SKIRT FRONT

CF

SCALLOPS

RUFFLE

# Morning Dress

## 1823–1827

This dress is made of white cotton percale, and partially lined in white linen under the arms. The front is darted, with the darts turned toward the sides; the front laps and is topstitched to the side pieces before the lining is added. The sides (with their linings) and backs are seamed with self-fabric piping, as is the shoulder strap to the back. The centre back fastens at the neckline and waist with hooks and eyes. The bodice is trimmed with a 5cm (2in) wide muslin ruche edged with two white cotton zigzagged tapes on either side, the whole placed between the broken lines on the front and back of the bodice. On the centre-front and centre-back edges of the trim a 12mm (½in) wide scalloped and embroidered muslin ruffle.

The sleeves are set into a piped armhole. The bottom of the sleeve is taken up in three horizontal pintucks, then the trim – two muslin ruches, separated from each other and the sleeve by double zigzagged tapes – and then finally a scalloped ruffle edging.

The skirt is topstitched flat to the bodice to the mark and then backstitched. The bottom of the skirt is trimmed with three pintucks, then three ruches separated from each other and the skirt by double zigzagged tapes. The lowest ruche is edged with double zigzagged tapes and a wide band of scalloped and embroidered muslin. The design of the embroidery is given at 6mm (¼in) scale: a flower picked out in eyelets with satin-stitched stem and leaves, with a row of eyelets along the edge of the scallop. The upper edge of the scalloped band as well as both edges of the ruches are hemmed prior to making up.

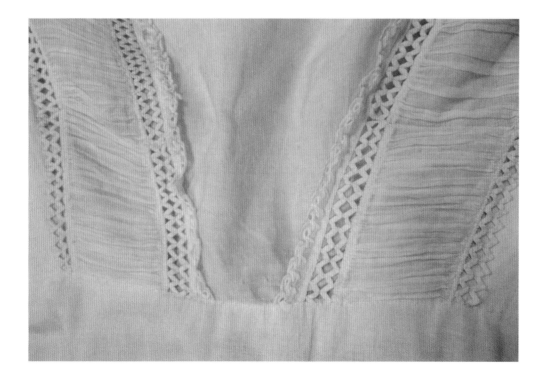

Left: *White cotton dress courtesy of the Historic Cherry Hill Collection, Albany, NY (3720). The front bodice is trimmed with muslin ruche.*

Right: *Blue pelisse with sleeves full to the elbow, button fastening and three tucks at the hem. Hand-coloured fashion plate for* Young Lady's Pocket Magazine *(1824).*

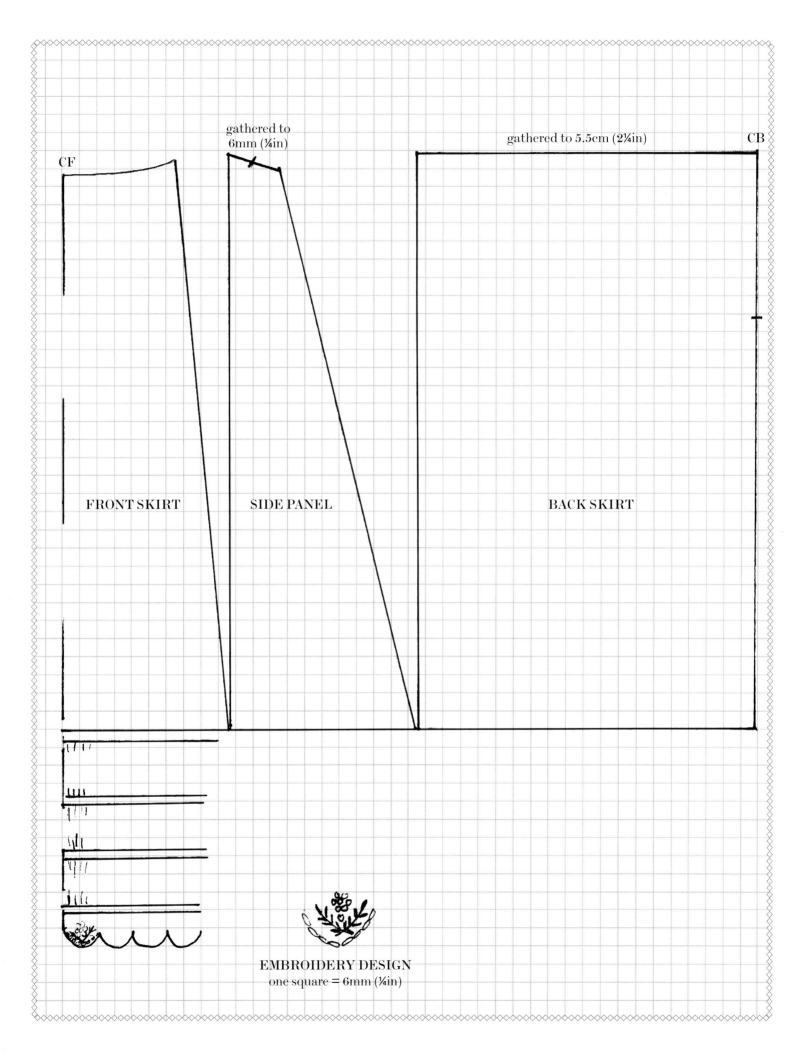

CF

gathered to
6mm (¼in)

gathered to 5.5cm (2¼in)

CB

FRONT SKIRT

SIDE PANEL

BACK SKIRT

EMBROIDERY DESIGN
one square = 6mm (¼in)

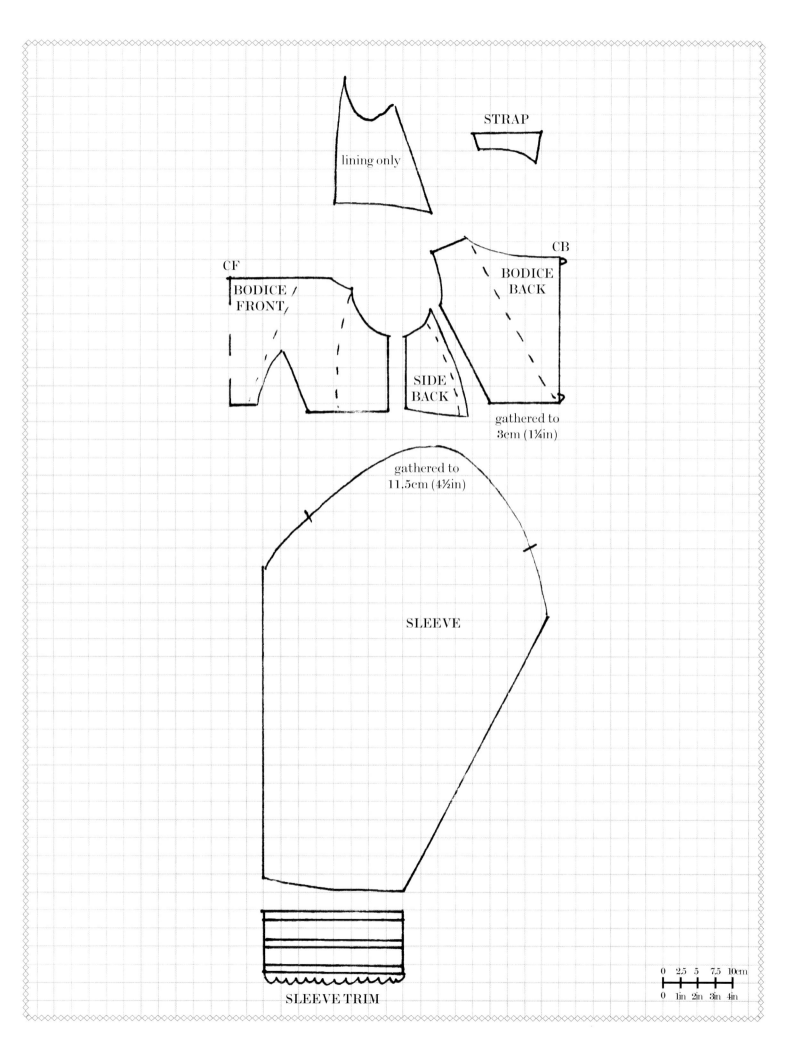

STRAP

lining only

CF

BODICE / FRONT

CB

BODICE BACK

SIDE BACK

gathered to 3cm (1¼in)

gathered to 11.5cm (4½in)

SLEEVE

SLEEVE TRIM

0   2.5   5   7.5   10cm

0   1in  2in  3in  4in

# Ball Dress
## 1824–1827

This ball dress of unlined gold silk crepe, which would have been worn over a white silk slip in order to better show the coloured silk embroidery, is said to have been worn by Elizabeth Douglas Monroe (see page 82) as a reception dress at her wedding in 1822. This is unlikely: the dress dates to several years after the wedding, and it would have only been suitable for an evening occasion, while weddings of the period were usually held earlier in the day. The embroidery has survived very well, but the delicate crepe has deteriorated to the point that the gown cannot be dressed on a mannequin.

The darts on the front are turned toward the centre and topstitched with ivory silk thread. The front is lapped over the back pieces and topstitched as well. The waistband, which is gold silk satin covered with crepe, is cut in three pieces, with the front lapping the backs, and is topstitched at the bottom of the bodice. The entire neckline is covered with an evenly pleated band (called *à la Sévigné* after a portrait of Madam de Sévigné), trimmed at every X with embroidered crepe tabs that are piped in satin. The band is pleated down to 5cm (2in) at centre front, 4cm (1½in) at the tabs on either side of the neckline, 4.5cm (1¾in) at the shoulder seam, and 3cm (1¼in) on either side of centre back. The bodice fastens at centre back with five hooks and eyes, and the waistband with two. The lower edge of the sleeve is bound with a bias band of crepe, and trimmed with a double box-pleated crepe frill with pinked edges, about 5cm (2in) wide. The armhole is piped.

The skirt is pleated as shown, and the whole backstitched to the finished edge of the waistband. Broken lines represent the areas of embroidery: the scalloped lines are brown vines with green leaves and pink, burgundy and blue flowers; the circles delineate large sprigs, each containing one of each coloured flower.

The broken line near the hem represents the lowest that any of the twigs or leaves from the vine dangle. There is no hem as such, but the crepe continues up the inside of the skirt to the vine, where it is held down and finished with the embroidery.

There is a separate belt of crepe over satin, the crepe embroidered in an undulating brown vine with green leaves and buds matching the flowers on the dress. One end is flat and holds three metal eyes; the other is pointed, with three hooks on the underside set several inches back from the point. The edges are piped in satin.

Left: *Dress courtesy of the New York State Historical Association, Cooperstown, NY (N221-1962). This detail shows the ornate embroidery on the skirt.*

Right: *A gown with an embroidered band of detail at knee level, corsage uni with horizontal revers, and cleft on the shoulders. From the simple style of the Empire dress at the start of the period to the fuller and more ornate dresses shown in this hand-coloured fashion plate from* Costume Parisiens *(1828), it is only a small step to the Georgian and Victorian confections that follow.*

Regency Women's Dress

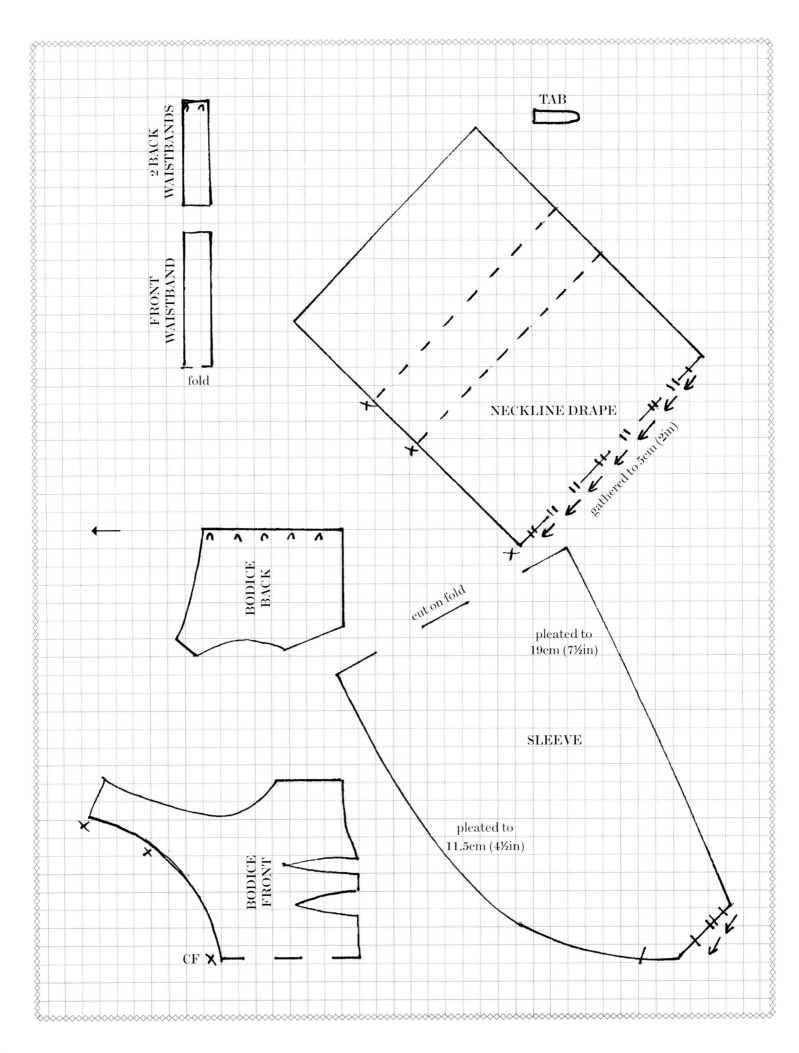

2 BACK WAISTBANDS

FRONT WAISTBAND

fold

TAB

NECKLINE DRAPE

gathered to 5cm (2in)

BODICE BACK

cut on fold

pleated to
19cm (7½in)

SLEEVE

pleated to
11.5cm (4½in)

BODICE FRONT

CF ✗

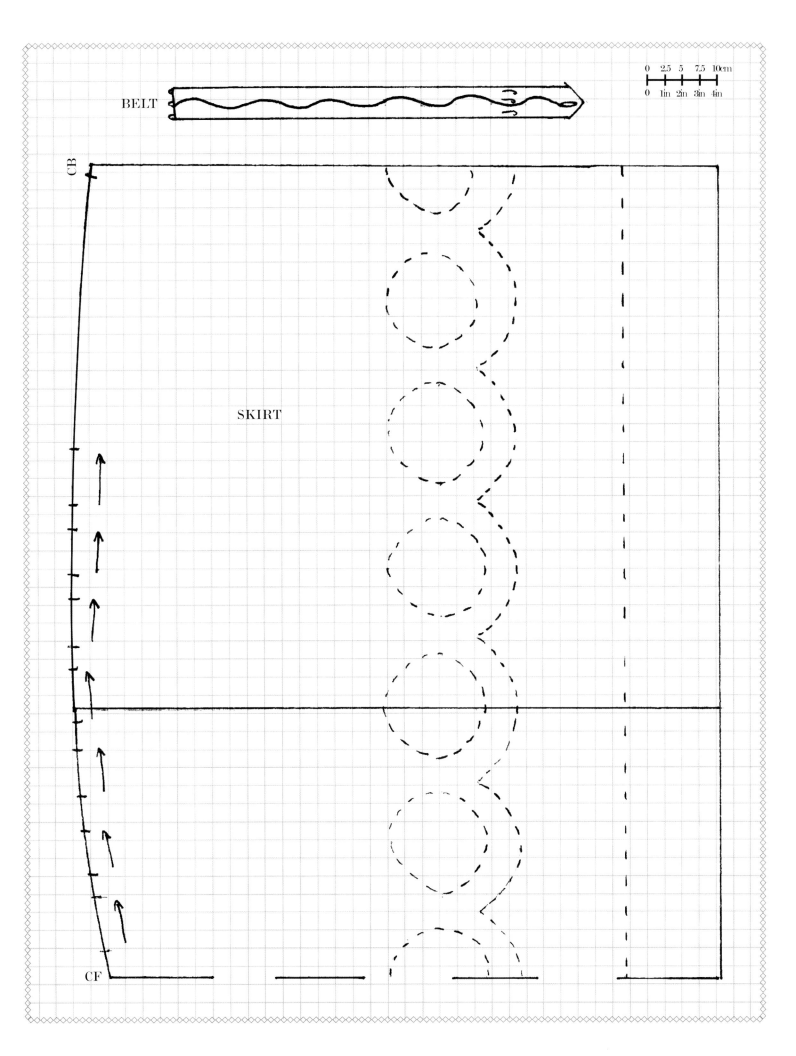

BELT

0  2.5  5  7.5  10cm
0  1in  2in  3in  4in

CB

SKIRT

CF

0  2.5  5  7.5  10cm
0  1in  2in  3in  4in

# Acknowledgements

I would like to take a moment to thank a few people. My parents and step-parents have supported me throughout the research and writing of this book, for which I am so grateful. My research was also aided by Kathryn Squitieri, who gave me access to the first twenty-odd years of La Belle Assemblée, without which I would not have been able to make numerous revelations. I also thank Kristy Richardson, my editor at Pavilion Books, who has done so much to get this book off the ground.

And, of course, very many thanks to the curators who allowed me to examine and pattern the garments in this book: W. Douglas McCombs, at the Albany Institute of History and Art; Deborah Emmons-Andarawis, at Historic Cherry Hill; Erin Richardson and Mary Alexander at the New York State Historical Association; Connie Frisbee Houde at the New York State Museum; Rebecca Beall, at Old Sturbridge Village; and Kathleen Coleman, at the Saratoga County Historical Association.

# Further Reading

Arnold, Janet, *Patterns of Fashion I* (Drama Publishers, 2005)

Barreto, Cristina, *Napoleon and the Empire of Fashion* (Skira, 2011)

Bradfield, Nancy, *Costume in Detail* (Quite Specific Media Group Ltd, 1997)

Friendship, Elizabeth, *Creating Historical Clothes* (Batsford, 2013)

Le Bourhis, Katell, *The Age of Napoleon* (Harry N. Abrams, 1990)

Johnston, Lucy, *Nineteenth Century Fashion in Detail* (Victoria and Albert Museum, 2009)

Waugh, Norah, *The Cut of Women's Clothes* (Routledge, 1968)

# Useful Addresses

## Museums

The Albany Institute of History
and Art
125 Washington Avenue
Albany, NY 12210
www.albanyinstitute.org

The New York State Museum
22 Madison Avenue
Albany, NY 12230
www.nysm.nysed.gov

New York State Historical
Association
5798 State Rte 80
Cooperstown, NY 13326
www.nysha.org

Brookside Museum
Saratoga County Historical Society
6 Charlton Street
Ballston Spa, NY 1202
www.brooksidemuseum.org

Historic Cherry Hill
523 South Pearl Street
Albany, NY 12202
www.historiccherryhill.org

Old Sturbridge Village
1 Old Sturbridge Village Road
Sturbridge, MA 01566
www.osv.org

## UK Suppliers

Devine Supplies
57a Brightwell Avenue
Westcliffe-on-Sea
Essex SSO 9EB

The Cane Store
Washdyke Cottage
1 Witham Road
Long Bennington
Newark
Nottinghamshire NG23 5DS
www.canestore.co.uk

MacCulloch and Wallis Ltd
25-6 Dering Street
London WIS 1AT
www.macculloch-wallis.co.uk

Whaleys (Bradford) Ltd.
Harris Court,
Great Horton
Bradford BD7 4EQ
www.whaleys-bradford.ltd.uk

## US Suppliers

Burnley & Trowbridge
108 Druid Drive
Williamsburg, VA 23185
www.burnleyandtrowbridge.com

Renaissance Fabrics
P.O. Box 5797
Concord, CA 94524
www.renaissancefabrics.net

Reproduction Fabrics
105 E Fourth Street, Suite 205,
Northfield, MN 55057 USA
www.reproductionfabrics.com

Timely Tresses
www.timelytresses.com

William Booth, Draper
2115 Ramada Drive
Racine, WI 53406
www.wmboothdraper.com

# Index